WHEN WILL IT END©

WHEN WILL IT END©

By Martin Tucker

1stBooks - rev. 02/14/00

ABOUT THE BOOK

My bout with religion started in kindergarten at age 5 and continued through grade school. At times, the attacks were fostered and encouraged by my teacher, Miss Gruber. In later years, it was determined that she was a member of the German-American Bund.

Most of my questions about religion and the hatred it bred as I matured were never answered.

My stressful life to survive the Great Depression was followed by World War II. I earned a Silver Star for engaging in five (5) major battles, including the Normandy Beaches and Battle of the Bulge – the two most memorable for Americans and the world.

The brunt of anti-semitism that dogged me in the Army, forced me into an anti-religion confrontation. As a result, I coined a phrase, "If you believe in prayer, pray that religion doesn't kill you." *When Will It End.*

I received General Patton's gift to the 5th Infantry Division, of which I was a part, for a bloody job well done, after taking the City of Rheims –never before divulged to the public.

Through the war, the warmth I felt that helped diminish the fear, the death, the constant horror, was the girl I left behind while not knowing if she would have me when I came home. Our seven-year relationship finally found us at the altar – not without insurmountable circumstances that we managed to conquer.

INTRODUCTION

This is a true story about Martin, who was one of many like him to bear the religious hate that followed him through his early years in school – followed by a bitter struggle to survive the years during the Great Depression of the 1930s, and who, with no respite, joined a lot of guys to fight a necessary war to save the world.

It was the hate festered in religion that for the past 80 years, had me constantly asking . . . **"When Will It End."**

From 1917 to 1945

PREFACE

It may be hard for anyone to imagine that my bout with religion and hate started when I was a five-year old child in kindergarten. It was so many years ago – yet while we remember some of the good things in our lives, the bad and ugly things are never forgotten. Even as a child, I saw the ugliness of religion that left its mark on me like a white-hot branding iron would have on my body.

I was in the third grade and had already been in fights with other boys in my class, just for being a Jew. I was too young to understand the question posed to the class by Miss Gruber, our teacher. "Who in this class believes in God?" My hand was one of the last to be raised. It was out of fear that I joined the other kids and raised my hand. I didn't hate the other kids because they weren't Jewish. I couldn't understand. Why was the question necessary?

Our circumstances at home while I was growing up, and the Great Depression of the 1930s, were both contributing forces that drove me to become a high school dropout. While we struggled to exist, World War II entered our lives. It all became my excuse for not continuing my education. More schooling may not have made any difference but I just may have felt a lot better about myself. The fear of a limited education kept me from putting my life's experiences into written words, but with the help of Webster's Dictionary and 80 years of learning in my world, I'll venture into the unknown.

I look around me, as I have so many times, for so many years, only to see a religious force wanting to scrap our "constitution" and make my country a "Christian United States." If that force were successful, assuming it were good, would it stop there? If that would happen, and given the opportunity, some would make our country all white if they could. Would it stop there? Since making the United States a Christian country is a possibility, I have to examine what life would be like in a religious government. Would it be a Catholic Christian government? Would it be a Protestant Christian government?

Would it be any of the many other Christian religions, who, in one fashion or another, differ with all the others?

Would a black person who is not a Christian, or a Jew, or an Oriental, etc. have to register our person? Would I, as a Jew, be exempt and accepted into the Christian society because the Orthodox Jewish Sect says the Conservative Jews and the Reform Jews are Gentiles.

From what I have read and from discussion, I'm able to define religion as a practice of "faith" – an invention by man based on fear. Look around us again: Christian killing Christians because (you know the ones who want to make this a Christian United States) one doesn't believe like the other. People of other "faiths" killing one another in the name of "religion" when they have no other reason. While a Christian force in my country, the United States is so busy trying to convert Jews to Christianity, the "Muslim World" is planning to convert the Christian world. What a horrible illness – out of control.

A friend, James, whom I met during my years in business, asked me a question one day as we sat eating lunch from a paper bag. "Whose God is right?" I was taken aback for some seconds. In addition to being an all around helper for the apartment complex he worked for, James was a Baptist preacher for his church. James couldn't help feeling second class only because he was black.

I hesitated and said, "If you're looking for truth and identity, you have yourself to blame. You criticize white people for your people's lives and rightfully so, but how in the world could you have accepted the white man's Christian god after you were brought here by them in chains, kept in ignorance, beaten and murdered, many times for nothing. Oh, some Christian whites would say now, just to make themselves feel good, it was wrong, while there are still those who would, if they could, send you back to Africa and some still look to exterminate you, as a sport. My personal feeling is that I'd have more respect for you had you chosen to worship and believe in a rock than the lack of enthusiasm you show for the religion you now embrace and question."

James was an intelligent man who had as much schooling as

I had. What he didn't have was an answer to what I just told him. As I left to keep an appointment, I turned to James and said, "If you believe in prayer, pray that religion doesn't kill you. When will it end?"

I remember, at school in our history classes we learned about the Crusades: an army of Christians led by the Pope. Those people responsible for what was written in our history books wanted and meant to glorify the killing and to brainwash the children into believing the Christians were right. Even in early films of Christians killing other helpless people, we in the audience cheered the Pope as he came down on his victim with his sword. It took many years to learn they were very wrong, wrong to kill, just because others weren't Christian.

When Christopher Columbus landed on these shores we call the Americas, and those who followed him with the "Cross of Jesus," their religious symbol, before them in the name of their Lord, they murdered thousands of natives. As kids attending our Saturday afternoon movie – there are still many of you out there who remember it well – the films of white American cowboys and the U.S. Cavalry killing American Indians, as the theater audience applauding and shouting approval while hoping there would be more. We believed our history books, written by people who wanted the children to grow up believing what the writers wanted them to believe. Look at the masses of people who surround the bible-thumper. Hey, I could bring you a message you'd love to hear that would be as good as any heard in the past 2000 or more years, for free. For money, I'd make your cup runneth over.

To many people, religion, like medicine, is helpful but you don't take the medicine if you don't need it. And like medicine, if you need it, you should be cautious as its effect sometimes can be deadly.

I was approached once and invited to join "Jews for Jesus." When I asked for a reason I should consider accepting, my host said, "because Jesus was a Jew." Since I don't accept any religious laws to govern my life, that reason was as empty to me as the religion.

We joke a lot about married life; joke about who contributed more to marital happiness, but I'm not joking when I admit that without my wife, Mitzie, there would be nothing of value in my life.

Mitzie doesn't agree with me about my nonreligious feelings. She does hesitate when the religious right or other religions sound threatening or she hears talk of religious wars. But then, Mitzie and I have agreed and disagreed for 52 years.

And then there was Mom. We hear so much about "family values." Mom never had one day of schooling and there were no diplomas to adorn the walls of her home, but her values as a mother, surpassed the experts.

Although I have used obscene language many times before, when I felt it was fitting, I apologize for some of the language I use in this story.

Chapter 1

I am 80 years old and still enjoy good health. If I dare to look to the years ahead, I hope Mitzie and I will celebrate many more birthdays and anniversaries together.

Even though many of the past years were rough, some even desperate, we must have done something right to still be in love and still caring for each other. I listen to her more than I used to, while still disagreeing with many decisions she makes for us. Mitzie is always ready to do things, ready to go places … sleeping isn't on her list. If I'm to believe "opposites attract," then I have to agree with the slogan.

I was 74 years old when my motivation to write this book began. Mitzie was saying again that I was getting in a rut and if I didn't snap out of it, I'd get in so deep I would never be able to join the human race again.

For many years of our married life, we couldn't afford vacations. Even traveling to nearby vacation spots was out of reach. Mitzie and I both worked very hard to overcome hardships that cropped up so often. We did manage in our later years to crawl out of poverty to what some people would call middle class. Thanks to Mitzie, we got to see some worldly sights and even got to see some of our own country.

We never had any children. I came from a small family; Mitzie's brothers and sisters numbered eight. I somehow knew Mitzie always wanted children, so the fault really was mine. Circumstances were always an important factor with me and even though I thought about children many times, I kept looking for the right time. Too many years went by and without any discussion, we just settled for one another.

Chapter 2

One of our disagreements stemmed from an invitation to attend an anniversary in Philadelphia that Mitzie said was important. I don't recall anything ever happening in the family that was so important that my being there or not being there would be noticed. Discussion about the anniversary lasted some two weeks before I gave in. I swore I would never again use the Auto-train, but again, Mitzie's wisdom, pointing out the saving of wear and tear of 900 miles of driving had me agreeing with *her. Like with the snap of a finger, the day to board the train was upon us, and as before, we never slept a wink for the entire trip. Although it wasn't planned, Rosaline, Mitzie's sister, arrived in Philadelphia at almost the same time as we did. Ro, as everyone called her, lived in Tampa, Florida, with her husband, Ed. Ed was too busy to make the trip with her but said he'd be along in a few days.

It had been many years since I was in Philadelphia. In visits before, circumstances kept me from touring the old city as I had wanted to. There were still several days before the celebration. Mitzie, Ro and Dorothy, another of Mitzie's sisters, decided to do some shopping and elected me to drive.

I was still familiar with the main streets of our old city but got fouled up when some road construction detoured us through some unfamiliar neighborhoods. I felt a chill as I turned into a street while glancing at the street sign, "Chew Street." Mitzie, Ro and Dorothy were so engrossed in conversation, they paid no attention to where we were, nor would it have mattered to them at all. You see, we were in my old neighborhood.

Had I planned this shopping trip, I would have been slightly prepared and there would be no tug at my heart such as I was having. I really wasn't listening while Mitzie kept repeating, "Stop here." She pointed to a yogurt sign on a store window, saying she, Ro and Dorothy would like some. I angle-parked facing the store and sat motionless and speechless.

As though I were coming out of a trance, I finally heard Mitzie say, "Are you all right?"

"Yes," I answered, and with what could be considered hypnotic movements, I walked into the store, bought three Yogurts, and as I handed them to the girls, I pointed to the Yogurt store and said, "I was born here." They blurted remarks of surprise at such a coincidence and finally understood why I was overcome.

"I would like to stay here for a while; would you mind taking the car? I'll get back to Dorothy's somehow." With Dorothy in the car, they could get around easily and not get lost, as Dorothy lived in Philadelphia and was familiar with most parts of the city.

I stood facing the store and dwelling, unaware they had driven off. The numbers above the private entry door – 432 – just to the side of the store's entry door, were as I remembered them so many years ago. The many coats of dark colored paint almost obliterated the numbers. The small storefront vestibule held the store's entrance door and also the private door that led to the upstairs dwelling. Once inside the entry and immediately to the left was another private door that led into the store, and then through the store into the downstairs living quarters. It came to mind how the winter snow drifts would pile up in the entrance covering the quart glass bottles of milk and newspapers that were delivered during the early morning hours. How difficult a job it was for Mike, our milkman, to fight his way through the many blizzards and freezing weather.

Unlike the door that led to the store with its clear glass, the private entrance door had on the inside a stretched lacy fabric over its partial glass front, keeping the view obscured to peepers. I looked up and down the street from the sidewalk and nothing, after all these years, seemed changed.

Having taken a grip on myself, I went into the store again, sat at the counter and asked for a Yogurt. The girl behind the counter, probably being security conscious, asked me why I was looking around the store. "I was born here," I said. She looked again at me and said, "Wow!"

I always thought I looked young for 74, since friends would say I did, and my ego would allow such compliments. The girl behind the counter recognized me for what she perceived I am, a

4

very old senior citizen; could that have been why she said, "Wow!" I was almost through my Yogurt and I knew even before I sat down that I would ask, and I did.

"Would you allow me to walk through the living rooms of the dwelling?" She said her name was Marge and there was nothing to see behind the center door that led to the old downstairs living quarters.

"This door has always been locked and I'm supposed to keep it this way." She hesitated again, and looking me over again a little more approvingly, said, "O.K." As she turned the key and the two slide bolts she said, "You can't go upstairs, people are living there."

Chapter 3

I shut the door behind me and stood so still. I felt I was possessed by a time machine waiting to be released.

Where I stood was our living room – the one small window looked out on the alley on the side of the house. Only a few steps away, I could see our old dining room. I still stood rigid, almost afraid to move. The rooms seemed so small. The dust was so thick everywhere and it seemed like no one ever lived here after we did so many years ago. The little bit of light coming through the dirty windows gave an eerie look and feeling to the empty rooms.

The dust on the floor left footprints as I walked to what used to be our dining room. The two small windows in the dining room also looked out on the narrow alley. Being so close, the house next door also kept much of the light out, adding to the dismal look. The kitchen was next and while taking such small steps, memories began to crowd my mind. The kitchen back door was nailed shut and I had to wipe the dirt from the door window to see the back yard. As a child I would play in this very tiny yard. Mom would forbid me to go beyond the gate. Mom had to know where I was every minute and that I was safe.

Beyond the yard was the large empty lot. The kids from the neighborhood and I used to play here . . . it helped at times to keep us off the streets. Parents found it easier to keep an eye on their children. Except for being overgrown with shrubs and weeds, it still looked the same.

I turned to look at the kitchen again – so much of growing up was in this room. As I turned to leave, the combined stark beauty and ugliness of this dust-filled place filled me with a wealth of warm memories. I started for the door leading to the store and began to live it all over again.

Chapter 4

It's February 11, 1917 and in the Jefferson Hospital here in Philadelphia, I'm being born. Even though my father is out in the hall by the door of the delivery room, I thought I heard him say, as I was entering the world, "It's bad enough that we might get in the war, now we have Martin.

It was a time when songs like "Alexander's Ragtime Band" and the Doughboy's song, "Over There" were so popular. Pop wasn't the happiest daddy with another mouth to feed while business was not so good. I heard some years later through gossip that I was an accident. However, I was accepted.

Pop was a paperhanger, and this ice cream store was once his showroom. A low, narrow ledge jutting from the front store window held rolls of wallpaper over a rack, displaying their designs and colors. In front of two well-placed chairs were three wallpaper stands. Pop would stand behind the display and flip page after page of sample papers for customers. When I was old enough to understand more, I realized it was a battle of confusion to choose the right wallpaper.

To the rear wall of our store stood Pop's roll-top desk, kind of hidden from a customer's view.

With three children and competition being a constant hurdle, Pop worked very hard to provide for us. We were Jewish and living in a community of Irish, German and Italian business and professional people. We lived in the town of Olney, in the northeast part of Philadelphia. It was almost impossible to tell when you arrived and when you left our town, since one community melted into another without distinguishing borders. Our store was just one dwelling away from the corner of 5th Street at Chew. From our store window you could see a police officer in the middle of the street intersection directing traffic. He stood and sometimes sat under a colorful umbrella with a stop and go sign atop the umbrella. In the center, atop the stop and go sign, was a lantern . . . a green side for go and the red side for stop, and inside the lantern, a lit candle that helped to show and guide the night drivers. With just the push and pull of a small arm, he would direct traffic.

Automobiles were the rage of the time. The Ford Model T was popular, although Pop had a Chevrolet Touring Car built by General Motors. It wasn't much different than the Ford. It was black, like most cars of the time, and cost about six hundred dollars. Pop needed the touring model because it was open on both sides and he could stretch his ladder and folding planks across the width of the car. On Sundays, the car became a family possession and we'd pile in to go visiting family and friends. Sometimes we'd just drive around town to see new sights. Because the automobile was new and expensive, we spent a lot of time cleaning and polishing it.

Even with automobiles increasing in number, the horse-drawn vehicles were still prominent as was the presence of the clean-up people with their tall pushcart cans that followed and cleaned up after them.

Almost from birth to my fourth year, I had every childhood illness. Some were contagious, so Mom kept me in the back bedroom on the second floor far away from Tillie, my sister, and my brother, Sam.

I had such a fear of our doctor, the sight of his black bag would start me screaming. Mom sat with me through many days and nights, and I think now how terrible it must have been for her to endure such hardships.

It was years later we talked about how, when I smiled, my front teeth hardly showed. A new doctor, one of many who had examined me, said one of my illnesses came from a diseased upper gum. I don't remember how I got to the hospital or how I got back home. I'm sure Mom explained how difficult I was as a patient . . . they must have drugged me. About ¼ inch of gum was cut away in the attempt to get rid of the diseased part. It all had to have happened some time between the appearance of my first and second growth of front teeth. I never heard, in general conversation during my childhood days, about laws covering unnecessary operations. There was, I'm sure, no way to know if this was one of them. Doctors guessed then what might be wrong, as they still do, and I suppose they will be guessing for years to come about many illnesses. Also, we can't always blame the doctor . . . in my case he may have been right.

Chapter 5

I'm four years old and I was beginning to leave all my illnesses behind me. I was growing stronger. Mom started taking me for walks and I was beginning to see our neighborhood for the first time. The most exciting sight of all was just two blocks from our home. A fire station, with a fire wagon that was drawn by six white horses. A black spotted dog, the firemen's mascot, who was sitting atop the wagon came down to meet us. I later learned the Dalmatian was appropriately named "Spot." I very cautiously petted him. A fireman sat me on the fire wagon and showed me the hoses and axes and other things they use when fighting a fire. The horses were in an adjoining stable.

I would sit in front of the store for hours, watching people go by and automobiles chugging up and down the street.

Timothy, the policeman on our street, was a big man, so he seemed to me, and I remember him as being very friendly. At Christmas time, my father always gave him a gift and many times through the year, Pop would give him a packet of cigars. I'm sure the other business people on his beat were also generous.

The fruit market on the corner, just a few steps from our store, was a favorite spot of Timothy's. Max was always tossing an apple or pear and Timothy was an expert catcher.

At the curb in front of our store was the street gas lamp. I was told, Philadelphia was famous for their gas lamp fixtures. At dusk, Luigi, carrying his ladder and stick, would climb up and with the crook in his stick and with a small torch, light the lamp. Luigi was a very short man, hence the ladder. You had to be up early in the morning to catch him turning off the lights.

In front of each store was a cellar door. Most times, even though a bar at the top was stretched across from side to side when open, they were kept shut to avoid the accident of anyone falling into the cellar. Just around the corner, Mr. Kleinman, the German baker, would open his cellar door in the morning and the aroma of fresh baked bread and cakes would fill the whole street.

Mom would take me by and I'd crouch down to peer into the cellar where the ovens were, to watch Mr. Kleinman at work. The aroma made me think I could eat everything he made.

As we walked further down the street, Mom pointed to the neighborhood movie theater. I was still too young to go, but my brother, Sam, told me it had only cost five cents for admission and if you only had three cents, they would let you go in for that. I'll get to see a movie some day soon.

Chapter 6

I was five years old and preparing to start kindergarten. What a break this was to be for Mom. Because of my illnesses for so long and constantly being by her side, I became inseparable and thought anything away from home a frightening place.

Hand in hand, Pop and I walked the two blocks to James Russell Lowell Public School to be enrolled and to spend the first morning of my first day of a strange new life.

I did not speak or understand a word of English. Mom and Pop both were immigrants. They escaped the poverty and the tortures of being Jewish in Russia. Like millions of others, they reached our shores in the most uncomfortable way anyone could imagine. Even though Pop spoke English very well, he had almost no schooling. Mom did not speak or understand English at all. In her old country she had no schooling. Yiddish was her language and for her sake and comfort, that's the language we all spoke at home.

Mom was quite learned in Yiddish. She could read and write and was just as worldly as we on many topics concerning current events. The Yiddish newspaper, "The Forward," was a daily and all events equaled the "Evening Bulletin," the "Philadelphia Inquirer" and the "Philadelphia Record." Many times there were items pertinent to Jews and international affairs that you would not find in our local newspapers. I don't know, but Tillie and Sam may have started school the same way I did. Obviously, they managed to overcome the handicap.

Being so close to Mom and Pop, I guess, was the reason I was so shy away from home. I stayed so close to Pop I was almost hugging his leg when Mr. Regar, the Principal, greeted us and, after being registered, escorted us to the classroom where I was to be left. Miss Gruber, the teacher we were introduced to, put her hand out to take mine, to take me to my desk. I drew back, grabbing Pop's leg. I began to cry while Pop tried to talk to me, to convince me everything would be all right. Miss Gruber started toward me and again was greeted by a chilling scream. The disruption was too much so Pop had to take me home. We repeated this attempt every day for a week, one day being worse than the last. A plan was arranged for Pop to stay in the classroom with me and after several days I became accustomed to the surroundings and it finally was safe to leave me alone. Since I was unable to communicate with the teacher, Pop told me, as he also told Miss Gruber, since I didn't understand English, that if I had to go to the bathroom, I would raise my hand. This happened the very next day and Miss Gruber, looking straight at me, ignored my hand waving. Was she punishing me for disrupting her class a few days ago? After a minute or so I lost control and the trickling sound and puddle brought laughter from the children around me. Miss Gruber let me sit there in my wet embarrassment.

Chapter 7

Four years went by and I was nine years old and in the fourth grade. I guess I learned quickly and well as English was no longer a problem. I liked school, but I couldn't tell why. I would come home and tell Mom all about my day and about the things I learned. That could have been a reason.

But problems hadn't ended for me by conquering the English language. It seems they were just beginning.

Our school day began with "Assembly." The room I was in like the others next to ours and so on down the hall, were connected by moveable sash doors. The six or seven sash doors rolled into a single group to one side of the room, making the four or five individual rooms into one large room. In one of the rooms there was a piano played by one of the teachers. Assembly began with a "Prayer" and the Pledge of Allegiance to the flag, then everyone sang songs. One song was "Dixie." Two other songs I was told by Jerry, one of my friends, were taken from his church hymn book. The final song of the morning was, as it was every morning, "Onward Christian Soldiers." I sang all the songs along with all the others, but when it came to "Onward Christians Soldiers" I did not join in.

In my childish way of thinking, the song offended me.

I used to listen to war stories Uncle Louis would tell. He was in World War I with many men of different religious faiths so if the song was to show patriotism it didn't belong only to Christians.

Pop used to tell me it would take many different people if you were to be successful fighting for freedom

The teacher in charge of "Assembly" was Miss Gruber. She was in charge every morning. She would walk between the rows of children swinging a short baton, in rhythm with the music. Since this was her routine every day I paid no particular attention. Suddenly, she was standing in front of me, staring. When Assembly ended and we were back in our respective room, Miss Gruber, who was also my room teacher, called me to the front of the class. She held a large ruler in her hand as she

17

walked toward me. "Hold out your hand," she said. I did and with that she came down with the ruler over the back of my hand with a scowl on her face. With an angry tone in her voice, she blurted, "Tomorrow morning and every morning I want to hear you sing "Onward Christian Soldiers." I returned to my desk thinking, "What's the point in singing a song about something that is meaningless to me? My friend told me they sing that song in church. What possible satisfaction could Miss Gruber or anyone have, except to have fed her pangs of hate. But why should Miss Gruber hate me? If this is a part of education, I just learned something. If it was Miss Gruber's intention that I must never forget this song, she has succeeded."

I didn't mention the incident to Mom or Pop when I got home; they would only worry about me and it would only be for nothing. I did think to myself, "Was Miss Gruber's God punishing me?"

The public spectacle Miss Gruber displayed came off as a message to some of the boys in my class. One boy, looking at me from his desk that was near mine, said "I'll get you for not singing "Onward Christian Soldiers." Some of the boys were bigger than I and what made matters worse, I was no fighter. They caught me at recess in the yard and when we returned to our room Miss Gruber walked to my desk, glanced at the bruise on the side of my face, then continued with the class as though nothing happened. Mom new what had happened the minute I came into the house. She said nothing and I said nothing. I thought to myself, she must have experienced this many times with my brother, Sam. Sam was four years older than I and having been in a situation like I just had, he must have learned what to do. Sam took me out to the yard to show me some defensive positions in boxing and one or two points in how to be aggressive. My lesson in fisticuffs was on a Friday afternoon and I was occupied the whole weekend with thoughts of what I might have to face on Monday when I returned to school. Maybe it's just in a kid's mind that bigger is stronger and how disadvantaged I am for being so small. Maybe just the thought of my opponent feeling superior gives him the edge over me. Will going to school every day be like this?

18

It was as though the whole confrontation was pre-planned.

As I walked to the place we were to file in line, waiting for the bell to sound, some of the kids began to gather. Richard, he's the one who gave me a bruised face last week, came from behind and shoved me, knocking me down. We both stood there poised with fists, one waiting for the other to strike. I could sense Richard was more confident than I was. Richard swung first at me and I ducked. The spectator kids had formed a circle and started yelling, "Beat the Christ killer. Kill the Jew." I suddenly realized what this was all about. It was about being a Jew in addition to not singing "Onward Christian Soldiers." The biggest boy in the class was chosen to fight me to assure the outcome of the fight. A fire within me erupted and all at once I became angry at everyone around me. I was trying to remember the things Sam taught me. Richard swung again, and again I ducked, but this time I came back almost unconsciously hitting Richard in the nose. He was bleeding and the kids supporting Richard quieted down, probably after seeing their hero standing there moaning in pain and crying while catching his blood in his cupped hands. Over all the shouting no one noticed that the bell had rung, but by this time Miss Gruber had come out to escort us to our room. She first took Richard to the infirmary while another teacher escorted us to our room. Minutes later Miss Gruber returned with Richard. His bleeding had stopped but he sported a very red nose. Miss Gruber, grabbing my ear, said, "We're going to the Principal's office." I couldn't help but think she could have been behind the whole thing.

I walked home slowly, thinking about the scolding I was going to get. I knew I had to tell Pop the whole story. He could see that I wasn't hurt, but he scolded me and he scolded Sam for his part, knowing in his heart, "we" didn't and we don't have any choice. After all, Mom and Pop had to run from a kind of life worse than that.

I'm guessing that under pressure from Miss Gruber Mr. Regar, the Principal, called my father to come to his office to confront him with the fight I had with Richard. We sat in Mr. Regar's outer office with Miss Gruber waiting for Mr. Regar's announcement to enter his office.

It was easy to see the hate in Miss Gruber's face – the effort she was making to make it as unpleasant for me and for Pop was obvious. It could have been the pain she exuded to bear the thought that the Jew who was so much smaller than Richard won the fight.

Mr. Regar's first remark was, "Such actions couldn't be tolerated," indicating I was at fault. Pop's street smarts were not expected when he asked to see Richard. When Richard came into the office, Pop asked permission to ask Richard a question. Mr. Regar, waving his hand, said yes. Pop asked Richard who started the fight and Richard started to blame the other boys who were around us. Mr. Regar could tell that Richard was trying to stretch the truth and interrupted, ordering Richard to tell the truth. After a long hesitation, Richard said, "I guess I did." Then Pop asked Richard to stand next to me. It was too obvious and no more was said.

Pop's quiet disgust was shattering. I could hear him say to himself, anti-Semitism. When we got home, a conversation between Mom and Pop ensued in their native tongue, Russian, about the whole affair. Of course, it was meant for me not to understand, but the timing and the tempo of their discussion could only have meant implications of anti-Semitism.

There were times when I heard Miss Gruber speaking to other teachers. When I told Pop that I was able to understand some of what was spoken, but wondered if Miss Gruber was Jewish, Pop said that it was German they spoke and that was why I only understood some of the words.

These children weren't born with hatred for anyone. Where did they learn to hate and with a vengeance to kill. My first thought would be, their parents. And they, as children, from their parents and so on. I would think, as God fearing and good Christians, as they all claim they are, they would have, through their church, made an effort to show the wrong in all this hate. I think at one time it did start and did come from the church handing it down to their people every day and especially on their religious holidays and they to their children at Sunday School teachings. I remember playing with the non-Jewish kids in the back lot behind our house. Religion talk happened to come up when one of the kids mentioned one of the "We're not allowed to…." "If we don't eat fish on Friday God will be mad and we won't go to heaven." Even in my ignorance as a kid this came across as pure stupidity. Again, if there were a real basis to religion, it would be more meaningful to teach children from something substantive rather than through fear.

I never heard any of the Christian kids and even adults say Christ was a Jew. It was once mentioned at the school playground and Christian kids would yell, "No, no." Well, you can't and you don't erase something by shouting, "no," like trying to erase the tiger's stripes or the leopard's spots.

I heard stories of other religious people that killed Christians only because they were Christians. Even Christians killing Christians. Hey, how stupid can you people be. What's a Jewish bewildered kid to think if this is religion. "When will it end."

Unfortunately, the fighting because I was a Jew was not the end of this episode. Different kids elected to pick on me and because of these confrontations I became a loner, always aware of who I was and always on the defensive and with each contestant I became a better fighter.

For many months, with almost each fight, Pop was called to the Principal's office. Often I left my opponent bleeding or running away. I would like to believe that some of my victories over the bullies was the reason the fighting finally faded away. In fact, some of the kids that tried to beat on me became friendly.

Chapter 8

At home, we were taught to respect everyone. Being Jewish meant nothing special for me. My daily routine was very much the same as the Christian kids. Mom and Pop were members of our local Synagogue, but never showed themselves as being very religious. They enjoyed, as we children did too, some of the customs Jews enjoyed for thousands of years. Friday night dinner was special. It was the Sabbath. Special holidays were celebrated. Who wouldn't partake of the special good foods and gifts some holidays were meant for? I did notice though how different Mom and Pop were from my aunts and uncles. They used fear to keep their children behaving by constantly saying to them, "If you're bad God will punish you."

I realize and remember that then, as a child, I did not have the knowledge or wisdom the years have taught me about religion. But, as a child with only a child's wisdom, a sense of right and wrong was distinguishable and evaluated only as a child. As I look back, I remember going to Friday night service with Albert, my neighborhood friend. It was a single family house converted into our community Synagogue. If you were unaware of the orthodox laws, you would, as we did, stand and watch and wonder why the men gathered on the first floor where the Ark and the services were orchestrated, while the women climbed the stairs to the second floor to keep them separate from the men. Pop tried to explain it to me in the best light possible, but he too felt, as I already did, that it was wrong to classify women under religious orthodox law or any law as second-class or no-class people.

Compared to others in the congregation, our family was poor. One disgusting thing that had nothing to do with religion happened during one of our High Holy Holidays. Pledges of money to cover the cost of maintaining the synagogue was an open audible forum. The stares and some remarks from the congregation that followed my father's tiny, by comparison, contribution was to me an ugly stain. It was enough for Pop to decide to quit.

Jerry, my friend at school, was Catholic. He would tell me about people in his family going to confession every week to tell God, through the priest, to forgive them of their sins. When I asked Pop why Jews didn't do the same, he said, "That's what the High Holy Holidays were about – that Jews were too busy to be bothered and decided that once a year should be enough to cleanse them of their sins, allowing them to go forth and do what they did all over again – and to come back next year, raise more money and repeat." Who invented this "ritual?"

Chapter 9

Our neighborhood was beginning to show a new face. While we were facing personal problems and just trying to live, Fifth Street, our main business street, was getting a face lift. The corner five cent movie theater was being torn down and a new and larger movie theater was to be built around the middle of the block. The news had already spread throughout Olney and beyond.

Our streets were sporting new electric lamps, so much brighter than the gas lamps, but I believe, for nostalgic reasons, the city did not remove the gas lamps. After all, they were a Philadelphia historic treasure that had been designed by Benjamin Franklin. Somehow, I feel I'll still be looking for Luigi, our faithful lamplighter. These are some of the beautiful things that will be lost forever.

Chapter 10

For many past months I noticed Sam joining Pop when Pop went to work. I recall the many times Mom and Pop would try to have a discussion with Sam about his future.

I don't know at what grade Sam dropped out of school. The many discussions Mom and Pop had with him trying to steer him to a useful life were in vain. Sam loved baseball and, as a player, was very good at it. It could be the times he should have been in school he was at the Wentz Olney ballpark. He played catcher as a substitute for the Wentz Olney team many times. There were occasions when Pop would take me to see some of the games that Sam played in. There, for only minutes, I felt I had a celebrity brother. Had he at least pursued this sport he might have made something of himself. But, like school and everything else, he turned up a failure. Sam had no knowledge or ability for anything, always turning down suggestions Mom and Pop made. It was loss of patience when Pop reluctantly insisted he be a paper hanger. I didn't find out until later in life that it took great skill to be a paper hanger. To be the kind of paper hanger Pop was, well, Sam will never be that good. If he pays attention he may at least learn how to make a living for himself. Mom and I were hoping that Sam would at least be some help for Pop because of his condition. In this case, the father and son relationship in the work field needed a miracle to survive. As parents, they were too easygoing for a son like Sam. However, with a lot of prodding, arguing and Mom crying, from despair, Sam finally became a paper hanger.

Chapter 11

Pop's illness, for I don't know how many years, was a well-kept secret from us. We knew of the many hot baths he would take seeking relief from pain, but we never associated them with the arthritis he suffered.

After many years of doctoring, at the cost of thousands of dollars, one of Pop's doctors suggested special bath treatments that had, in many arthritis cases, helped reduce the swelling and relieve much of the pain. It was a convalescent home in Mt. Clemens, Michigan that advertised through doctors of their mineral baths. They prescribed three baths a week for four weeks, along with other treatments, during a patient's stay.

By now most of the savings were gone. Talk about paying for Pop's trip and having to hire a paper hanger to do the necessary work with Sam assisting was the main topic around the house. I had heard the word "mortgage" before and I knew it was one way people borrowed money so this was now the only way Pop could have one more chance at feeling, once again, like a useful person. It was done and Pop was on his way.

I don't remember what day it was, but this day was to be one worthy of celebration. Mom uttered some words that were unmistakably English. We were sitting around the kitchen table at dinner time, talking about doing whatever we could in the store to keep the business operating while Pop was away. Sam said he could stand by the sample wallpaper stand and flip the pages for a customer. Mom cleared her throat, meaning to get our attention, and then said, "I can do that." It was a tremendous surprise for us all. Mom seemed a little nervous and maybe surprise at herself a bit to bravely say something in English. She began to explain, in Yiddish, how she would sit at the desk in the store, obscured from the customers out front. She watched Pop and listened. I have often been told those two words were the secret to learning. It was also during the hundreds of times Sam, Tillie, Pop and I would ramble on in conversation in English while Mom, without us even noticing or paying attention, would be there listening and, in her own way, learning. Truly, a great

29

victory. I made a great effort from that day on to speak to Mom in English when possible.

During the four weeks Pop spent at Mt. Clemen's Convalescent Home, Sam worked with Paul, the hired paper hanger.

Much to our amazement and pride, Mom showed her skill a number of times in the store. After all, women in business in those days were rare and I watched many times and could see that customers liked her. Many customers were immigrants too, like Mom, with different accents and dialects. But Mom and the customer always seemed to understand and were comfortable with each other.

The four weeks seemed slow to end, but Pop is home and the sulphur baths helped a lot, or so it appeared. I really think Pop hid his nagging pain and went to work.

Chapter 12

There were people in the store for the longest time talking to Pop. Pop came into the kitchen where Mom was making a chocolate layer cake – no one since has been able to duplicate it. The people he was just talking to in the store were from the 1927 New Colony Theater that was to be built. They were hiring Pop to wall paper certain important areas of the theater. In addition to it being a well paying job, I felt a small glow of pride that we were going to be a part of this important occasion. Mom's smile turned into a frown. She knew from other theaters she had gone to that the walls reached dangerously high. Even for a well person, this needed a lot of careful thought before accepting the job.

She knew the scaffolds Pop would have to work on would be high. She knew too that even with the extra help on this job, Pop would not ask anyone to climb these heights. Not having been able to work for such a long time, Pop felt, as the family's provider, his duty to at last contribute what he always thought was his place to do. Money in the family's piggy bank was very low and that was another reason and Pop's prime decision to take the job. I will help as much as I can though Mom insisted I think of nothing but school. Her fear of my getting too close to wallpaper, etc. would rub off.

Chapter 13

Tillie has been seeing a beau for some time now, and it's beginning to look like there might be a wedding. It may appear to sound a bit callous, but my feeling is "GOOD RIDDANCE." I'm still considered a kid, but accepted or not, I'll speak my piece. In the latest of our one-on-one conversation, Tillie and I talked about the wedding. I insisted she go off, get married and telephone the news home. "There's no money for this, no matter how small we make it. After all we have gone through here at home, there's no gaiety looking forward to this marriage that you choose to do now." It looks like my brother and sister have grown up to be "me people" – not that they wouldn't do for me or Mom or Pop if asked, they just never made an effort to volunteer anything even if it was the right thing to do. So maybe a girl does need more guidance and care. I remember Mom and Pop deciding piano lessons would help give her confidence in addition to the pleasure it could bring knowing how to play an instrument. The same effort was afforded Sam to learn to play the violin and what a waste it turned out to be.

A twelve-volume set of the "Book of Knowledge" to help with school and homework finally ended on a shelf to become part of our dining room decor. Maybe I'll find a use for these books.

So much went into a tremendous effort to make Sam and Tillie good, solid and independent people. I'd like to think that Mom and Pop didn't make any mistakes although they could have saved a lot of money. The mistakes were made by my brother and sister. They were afforded opportunities and didn't know what to do with them. My advice was partially taken and a wedding reception was at home with just a family gathering.

Chapter 14

In 1928 Pop completed the Colony Theater job with bandaged hands and arms. I don't know how he managed it. We didn't want to think it, but it was to be Pop's last job. His arthritis flared up and like I always suspected, it never left him for a minute's peace.

Out of desperation Pop submitted to a family decision to go to a faith healer recommended by friends and other family members.

Pop was a non-believer of this method of healing, but again with nothing to lose, he gave in and agreed to this voodoo medicine.

We entered the faith healer's house, somewhere in South Philadelphia. Label, the faith healer, escorted us to a dingy, almost dark room which was enough to scare anybody out of the house and neighborhood. Pop kept asking questions and Label never answered him. Pop looked at Mom and me, standing at the other side of the room and said he thought we should leave. Mom said, "No." Label put his hands on Pop's arms and looking at the ceiling with eyes shut, uttered some sounds and swung his head in a circular motion. Label did this exercise three times, then dropping his head forward, holding that position silently for about a minute.

I thought, "What a performance." I'm glad we didn't leave. This was a once-in-a-lifetime experience.

Label told us to return in two days for the bucket size batch of salve he had to make. All that with instructions for $25. I guess when you've come to the end of the road as Pop had, one more try can't hurt.

The salve was black-like tar. The smell was horrible and for weeks the house reeked. Because of the pain in his hands Pop was unable to smear the salve on the strips of bandage Mom made from old bed sheets. I took turns with Mom to prepare the bandages. Only once did I see Sam pitch in. It must have been the smell that drove him away.

Chapter 15

Eleven years old Sixth grade.

Through word of mouth and local advertising, the announcement of the opening of the Colony Theater began making the entire community very festive. A Friday night was chosen as the most appropriate time for the celebration. Mom and I prepared ourselves in order to get a good standing spot along the curb to witness the gala event. We felt a little more than just spectators because Pop had a hand in putting on finishing touches that made this theater beautiful. With a large crowd gathering, Mom and I were still able to get a spot right across the street facing the front of the theater. A band had assembled in the center front of the theater sidewalk while, to the right of the band, were two large Kleig lights. Their beams streamed skyward for people far off to know something great was happening here tonight.

There were vendors all around with their stands, selling hot dogs, soda pop, ice cream and other goodies. The Mayor of our town and other dignitaries made speeches and announced the first talking movie made will be shown at the Colony Theater on this opening night. Pop had to be feeling very bad to have stayed behind. He would have enjoyed seeing all this. On our way home we stopped at Mr. Kleinman's bakery to bring some cream puffs for Pop and me and to tell Pop about the whole affair.

Chapter 16

The newspapers and radio were blasting the news of the stock market crash. I looked around me almost satisfied that such a terrible catastrophe couldn't touch us. How can you lose nothing I thought. I was very wrong.

Koslofsky, our next door neighbor, was a Realtor. His investments in property were being taken away. He was desperate.

Dr. Wallowitz, our dentist, was in a panic too. His office and living quarters were in the apartment above Max's fruit store. Although he was quite successful, he had patients he trusted and now was hoping he would be able to collect what was owed him.

I tried to understand the effect the stock market was having. What would I know about the market? I took no solace when hearing that the experts didn't know much either.

Factories and businesses began shutting down. People were losing their jobs, some losing their homes. The little business there was for us was now being done by Sam.

Pop had made several loans from the bank in the few years past, using our property for collateral. Along with the market crash came the bank's demand on the loans. The property was all that we had and it looked like we were going to lose it.

I took a part-time after school job at Max's fruit store. Max couldn't help but see our hopeless struggle and made the offer to me out of sympathy. I did what I could and more to show my appreciation. Even for Max, the market crash and its effect played havoc with his business. The lack of customers caused him to throw away lots of fruit and vegetables that had spoiled by the end of the day. There were times Max gave me some almost spoiled fruit and vegetables to take home. That and the $4 at the end of the week made me feel like one lucky kid.

A new word for me that I learned from the "Evening Bulletin," one of Philadelphia's newspapers, was "depression." It was a beginning of life I was to experience.

Chapter 17

For a kid my age it doesn't mean anything to find yourself in the middle of a political presidential race for the White House.

Even as kids we do understand right from wrong. We just don't know "who" is right and "who" is wrong. The polling place was down the street, in a store next to the Colony Theater. I walked down with my Mom as she was going to vote. Did I mention, Mom and Pop became citizens many years ago. Herbert Hoover, the Republican, was running against Democrat Al Smith - or maybe the other way around. Pop used to say President Coolidge, who was leaving office, was a do-nothing President and to have another Republican in office would be an extension of Coolidge. Pop was a registered Democrat, but he always said he'd vote for the best man, not the party. That sounds sensible, "but" ..... in politics, what does sensible mean?

There were a lot of people milling around the entrance of the polling place, from the doorway to the curb, so many that they blocked the path of people wanting to walk by. Mom and I stood at the curb for awhile. As we started for the front door a man from the crowd, with his hand up to stop us, offered Mom $5 to vote for Hoover. She refused and we went into the store for Mom to vote. When we got home Pop greeted us with the same story about someone coming in the store and offering $5 for a Hoover vote. The big Hoover cry was, "a chicken in every pot and two cars in every garage." As a kid that sounded good to me, but could Hoover deliver a promise like that? I had another problem I just couldn't figure out. It was during the presidential campaigning in the newspapers and on the radio that commentators were saying Al Smith didn't have a chance because he was Catholic. I knew from my school playground fights that Catholics hated Jews. So why should Mom or Pop vote for Al Smith? Hoover might have been a Protestant and it was no secret that Protestants hated Catholics and Jews. The newspapers and radio were constantly reporting the killing that was going on in Ireland which was news that affected this presidential race. Protestants were desperately trying to keep

Catholics out of the Government. I can see the dilemma here for Jews. There are more of "them," but let's look at this mess..... The Protestants and Catholics, with the same Cross of Jesus as a symbol of their God, were each claiming that God is on their side and praying feverishly for his side to win. I can't figure out why one godly group would want to kill off the other godly group. Quite confusing for their God (if there's only one), to decide who's side to take. I wondered who or what they are praying to. Like the kids in my fourth grade class who gathered around to see the supposedly Christ loving boy kill the Jew and then to grow up and kill one another. I need a lot of help understanding. When I asked Mom and Pop, Pop's best answer was that his parents and he too were still trying to understand.

Chapter 18

My 13th birthday was quieter than for most kids in Jewish families and I was glad that no fuss was made. It's another Jewish custom that may have meant something once upon a time when a boy became a responsible person.

I tried making graduating from the eighth grade an ordinary thing, knowing the hardship Mom and Pop were experiencing with Pop's illness that was also eating away at whatever money was left.

It was apparent that nothing more could be done for Pop and with the possibility that his condition could worsen, the future began to look very bleak.

My sister and brother didn't seem to be concerned. Their thinking may have been, "We can't do anything about Pop's problem." I respected them at first; they were older and I always looked up to them. They were my family, but it was also apparent that they were selfish.

Chapter 19

I was now off to high school. My sister and brother never made it, so my fantasy was to make it for the family. I had a slight good feeling about giving back something for 13 years of being a burden, but that's four more years away, if I make it. This would be a good time to push a magic button to make the time fly. Fantasy and wishing – fitting words.

I don't know exactly how much money is available and Mom keeps saying not to worry. It was on Sunday morning one week, before we must move out of 432 Chew Street, when Mom asked me to go with her to South Philadelphia. We arrived at a store that sold fabric and other notions for sewing and dressmaking. Mom didn't say why we were here or who she wanted to see. I figured she just wanted to visit a friend.

We walked to the back of the store, through a curtained doorway, to the living quarters of this woman's dwelling. I only remember the woman as being rather big with a large pimple on the side of her cheek. It was seconds later I saw Mom take the small diamond ring from her finger as she asked the woman how much she would give her for it. I remember how I felt, watching. I knew Mom had steeled herself for this, her only valuable possession. I also knew at this moment that there was no money. Why else would she part with the ring.

Fifty dollars was all the woman offered and, without a doubt, the ring was worth lots more. We hardly talked all the way home. We rented a house just one block away from our old place. $25 went for that and two men took $10 to move our things to the old new house on 5th Street. At a last minute deal Mom sold the piano. She never told me, but she couldn't have gotten very much for it.

Pop's condition is worsening. His fingers have swollen to twice their normal size. Even without him touching anything, his pain is unbearable. Mom has been managing as best she could with the little money there was to manage. One very important item we must always have is pain killing medicine for Pop. I sometimes think his pain pills don't do any good, but we must continue with them. I bristle with anger when I think of the thousands of dollars the doctor took from Pop, knowing they couldn't help him and then telling Pop there wasn't anything they could do when they learned he had no more money.

Being struck by lighting would not have been as shocking as was Sam's announcement that he was getting married. We had never heard of him being interested in anyone. He never mentioned seeing anyone. I was furious. He knew how serious conditions were at home and when I said how badly we needed his help, no matter how little, he said he couldn't help it. He made no further explanation. We hardly ever hear from Tillie and now with Sam gone, I'm frightened and despair has gripped me. the slim hope of help I thought would come from Sam was gone too.

Chapter 20

We had been living in this rented house on 5th Street for only six months when for lack of money we are forced to move again. I would guess we were five months in arrears of paying the rent.

Mom and Pop had never even thought of looking to relatives for help. They too were depression victims.

Pop had a cousin who lived in a part of Philadelphia called Feltonville, on Wyoming Avenue just above D Street. It was only about three miles away so Mom and I walked to Cousin Rose's house. I found myself calling her Aunt Rose for no reason and it stuck. Uncle Jacob, Aunt Rose's husband, their daughter, Reba, and Eugene and his wife were already living in this house. "Desperation" has its way of taking charge. Mom had no choice;' Aunt Rose, knowing our circumstances, was anticipating our visit and insisted we stay with her. It was very uncomfortable for everyone. We tried our best to stay out of everyone's way. Mom and I would take long walks, sometimes even in the rain, so that we would not contribute to the crowding.

He didn't know it, but in his silent pain I caught Pop crying, a sight even to this day is painful to me.

We noticed from time to time strange couples coming into the house. Aunt Rose would greet them and usher them upstairs to the second floor. Mom knew why and struggled with an explanation when I asked her what was going on. I wasn't completely ignorant of life, but I didn't understand these actions.

Halfway through Mom's explanations, I saw the light and stopped her, saving her any further embarrassment. Aunt Rose was performing abortions. Mom was extremely upset. Aunt Rose was a very bright, good and considerate person. She knew how uncomfortable this made Mom and wanted to save her from feeling she was part of this just by living under the same roof so Aunt Rose gave Mom enough money to rent a small house only a few blocks away. It was to be a temporary solution and, again, the choice was made for us. The few pieces of furniture we still owned were taken out of storage, thanks again to Aunt Rose.

We once again were on our own, apprehensive, but feeling better not having to watch what went on in Aunt Rose's house. We were now living at D and Courtland Streets, a row house, like most Philadelphia houses, and just three miles from Olney High School. It's a short walk for a healthy guy like me; a little tougher in winter I guess, but I'll survive.

Shortly after the movers left, Mom and I walked to the corner of D and Wyoming, just two short blocks from our house. We introduced ourselves to Ben Miller of Miller's Pharmacy. He was quite conciliatory after hearing about Pop. "Call me Ben," he said, "I'll do whatever I can to help."

We shopped prudently for food with the little money that was left from Aunt Rose's generosity. A week had gone by. I awoke this morning like I did other school day mornings; the usual lunch bag that Mom always had ready for me on the kitchen table wasn't there.

Mom was always close by every morning to say goodbye. This morning she didn't come downstairs and, after checking the icebox, I knew why. There was no food in the house. I called to her and Pop, "See you later this afternoon."

I got home from school about 3:30 PM. Mom was not around and Pop did not know where she was. She only told Pop she was going out and would be back later in the afternoon. It was 6 o'clock and I was trying to decide what to do about Mom when the front door opened and she walked in.

I looked her over to be sure – I don't know for what. Mom said, "I'm all right. I got a job." I was just getting over the anguish of her not being home and now I'm stunned at what I heard. I'm sure in the 15 years past and before, Mom had never been away from home alone. Mom said she was given directions to the factory were she'll be working and came home by similar directions. I was still very upset about Mom being out alone for so long, but more upset now that Mom will be going to work – to work for Pop and me. How much more of her should we take? Pop, silently, was terribly upset. His choices had run out. How terrible he must feel.

In a newspaper article that was also announced a number of times on radio, surplus cheese and butter was available at

48

government stations. Neither Mom or I could get ourselves to submit to this, but again, with no food in the house, it was our only choice. The lines were long, but I stayed with Mom while waiting our turn. We chatted and it helped pass the time. This will always be a day I'll never forget.

Chapter 21

Mom was going to be a sewing machine operator for the Lerner Blouse company. They're manufacturers of ladies blouses and other ladies light apparel and located at 40 North 6th Street in downtown Philadelphia.

On her Singer Treadle Sewing Machine we had at home, Mom had for years made clothes for us kids, dresses for herself, for Tillie and now and then a couple of shirts for Pop. She was good, but the machines she would be working with now are all power driven and all together different. She would have to learn all over again. It took some gut wrenching getting used to, watching her go off in the morning about the same time I'd go off to school. We both worried about Pop being alone, but again, no choices. I'd be home by 3:30 every day to do what I could for Pop. His day was not only long, but in the quiet and emptiness of the house his pain must have been even more unbearable. I guess his mental feelings added to his worsening condition.

Weeks faded into months and Mom conquered any and all anxieties. Her hard week's work brought her $8; it bought food, paid the rent, electric bill, but most of all, Pop's pain pills. From time to time, Mom would bring work home; like turning belts and collars. After dinner and my homework, Mom and I would sit around the dining room table and work on these, sometimes till midnight. At a penny apiece, sometimes two cents each, we made a little extra money.

I wasn't doing too well in school. I found myself blaming my failure on my preoccupation with home conditions – the truth being I'm just not smart enough. When I mentioned quitting school, Mom, in her soft and gentle way would say "No."

The depression didn't hit everyone severely. In other families both parents went to work (if work could be found) and their incomes were big compared to the money Mom earned. Some of the kids from homes like that had it a little better than I. Even though some of these kids were my friends, I couldn't join them for a movie or even a soda at the neighborhood drugstore.

51

Once in awhile, we'd get together at someone's house to play some records and just talk. Many times, from her skinny purse, Mom would hand me some money to join the other kids, but I'd say I don't feel like going out. I always hoped she didn't think something was wrong with me.

I spent many hours after school with a group from school that we formed to help one another with our school work. One member of the group, Paul, was a bright fellow. Learning seemed to come easy for him and he volunteered to coach us in subjects we found difficult. I tried so hard, but to no gain. Thoughts of quitting school had run through my mind many times. Mom sensed it and without any discussion would, from time to time say, "You must stay in school."

Several months passed and I now was past 16. One night at the dining room table while we were turning belts we had a long and soft spoken talk about me leaving school. It was for her the most difficult "yes" she ever said. It was the constant everyday pursuit that forced her to say yes.

It didn't take much to see how tired Mom was; I always worried about her getting sick. How would I know? She would never say.

I remember being critical of Sam and Tillie for being nothing without an education. They had every opportunity and threw it away. This was a different time with little or no choice. But here I am, also unprepared to face my future. I softened the disappointment for Mom by promising to continue with night school as soon as our situation began to look better.

Chapter 22

My Uncle Hyman worked for a food market at 17th and Venango. He was a butcher. I wasn't too fond of him, but I never let it show. With the loss of a couple of others in the family I thought it best for Mom's sake not to make waves so that she would have some family near. Uncle Hyman became acquainted with the people across from his store who ran a deli and some groceries, beer and soda. Mr. Nathanson said he could use a young man to do menial chores. I was hired at $5 a week. I opened cases of canned foods, jars of other foods, stacked the shelves, hauled beer and sodas from the cellar and kept them refrigerated and cleaned up the store. I was going to make the best of this job starting with learning the names of different cold meats and cheeses and how to identify them. I watched how sandwiches were made. I often made sandwiches at home for myself. It doesn't look any different here, but if it is, I'll learn. $5 a week isn't much. It will help. There never was anything left for the tiniest luxury.

Roosevelt was president at this time. His programs to get the economy going were just being introduced … if they work, we, way down here near the bottom of despair, won't know it for some time.

I worked for Mr. Nathanson for about a year. My eagerness drove me to learn all I could. It was through a friend that I was interviewed for a job at North City Delicatessen at Broad Street and Olney Avenue, not too far from my old neighborhood. The job title was Sandwich and Salad Platter Chef. It was touch and go at first, but after the first week I was good. I was never hungry here and managed at times to take home some things we couldn't keep for the next day's customers. My $15 per week brightened our world beyond description. The deli stayed open until 4 AM and for the longest time I worked the 7 PM to 4 AM shift. It was my first experience with night people and, luckily, the police on our street were around most of the time. I had my share of escorting some trashy guys to the curb who would stroll in.

There were regulars. Almost every night the same people would come in. I got to know them well enough to have their favorites ready for them. Three of our regulars were guys who looked to me like mob people. They would come in about 1 AM. Almost each time it was corned beef on rye with Russian dressing and a beer. I would serve them in their booth, never saying a word. On one of their visits they introduced themselves as Chick Adams, Max Aisen and Joe Seeby. Max spoke first saying that I had his job and that he used to work here at North City Deli. My first thought was that I didn't want to tangle with these guys if he thought I took his job from him. "You can have it back anytime, " I said. They laughed and over the next eight or ten months we got to know one another quite well. They weren't mob. Just three regular guys. Mr. Altshaw, the owner of the North City Deli, began missing work more often and after a short illness, he died. His family took over the business. Rumor had it that because of dissension in the family the business was to be sold. They did sell and the new people, having another family arrangement, had to let the old employees go. I was almost relieved at losing my job. I didn't care for it and I didn't want to get stuck with it for my future, but I'm going to miss that $15 weekly since I have no way of replacing it. Mom, I know, will say it's all right and we'll manage.

This is the answer to no education ... just flit from one poor paying job to another. What am I saying? Those were Mom's words.

Chapter 23

It was suggested by Pop's doctor that we put Pop in a hospital for a two week routine examination. With certain new-found drugs he would be better off and maybe more comfortable than at home. He seemed anxious to go, but I believe his reason was that he couldn't stand seeing Mom going off to work every morning. He was to be a test case and, of course, it was free. Also, with his advanced type of arthritis he was the right candidate for these new drugs. His was rheumatoid arthritis that by now had spread to his elbows and knees and the joints in his fingers were swollen to twice or more their normal size. It was almost as painful to watch him.

Watching Pop deteriorate was leaving its mark on Mom.

For the next two weeks I stayed close to Mom and tried to help occupy her time while waiting for results of Pop's new treatments and experiments. We took long walks and talked. Subjects ranged from family characters to rehashing her experiences at the Lerner Blouse company and mine from past jobs. We visited Pop many times during those two weeks. It was the opinion of the doctors that Pop's condition was in such a deteriorating stage that the new drugs had no relieving effect.

Chapter 24

Mom's main problem, and it may have been so for the longest time, was me. For a non-educated immigrant so far removed from this modern world, her thinking could be matched with the experts. She said she thought if I were interested and liked the idea I could get involved in the garment industry. Somehow she knew that circumstances wouldn't free me to return to school and she too wanted me to latch onto what could be a more promising enterprise. There was no argument against it. I wouldn't know if I'd like it unless I tried. Mom was way ahead of me. She had spoken to Mr. Maranoff, one of the Lerner Blouse company's partners, and he agreed to hire me.

In this very large room were rows of work tables that stretched some 50 feet and I counted ten such tables doing this work. My job was tying these small, sometimes large, bundles of parts of a garment. Collars, sleeves, belts, fronts and backs of different colors and sizes, then put into a cart and rolled to the rear of the factory to the Sewing Department. I'd move from one table to another to continue this operation. I'd carry large bolts of fabric from the fabric stock room to some of the tables for the cloth spreaders who were also the cutters.

At the end of the day, after the cutters would go home, I'd stay to sweep up the floor. The cutters being union men, worked five days a week while I returned on Saturday to work in the Shipping Department. All this for $6 per week. Many times I'd be sent into the Shipping Department during the regular work week to help box the finished blouses. This was after my eight hours in the Cutting Department. Management would give me 25 cents for supper. Their generosity was overwhelming.

Down the street and around the corner was the Automat and one of my favorite foods was a fish cake, spaghetti and a roll, all for 20 cents. The five cents I had left wasn't enough for any of the desserts so I saved the nickel each day from Monday to Thursday or Friday to buy the slice of cherry pie and a cup of hot chocolate. My other favorite drink through the week was water.

The year at Lerner Blouse company seemed to go by

57

quickly. I watched the other people at their respective jobs from the designer to the pattern maker to the cutter, all the way down to the sewing. When I thought no one was looking I would operate some of the cutting machines. It wasn't as easy as it looked and was somewhat dangerous. I would save some of the discarded paper patterns and at home I'd figure out how to grade the different sizes. Mom had an old size 10 dress dummy and, over time using the usual muslin fabric, I taught myself to design and drape the figure in order to create a garment. It must have been the pleasure I got from creating something that made me stick to this industry with the hope I'd be successful at something. To be good at this was still a long way off. In the meantime, it was back to my minimal job. I apparently had done my job well these past months to earn a dollar raise.

The depression still dominated nearly everyone's life. Many people were still out of work and, because of that, like in almost every industry, we were faced with a closed shop – no new members until the old bench warmers at the union hall got a job. I could by now do a cutter's job as well as any of the older, more experienced men, but because of the "closed shop" policy, I was unable to apply for a better job.

Al Gerber, the Shop Steward, and I were good friends by now, but every time I brought up the subject of becoming a union member he would say his hands were tied. Around town were a number of non-union shops that were constantly being picketed. Union people, some on their day off, and other unemployed union people from our industry would walk with placards up and down the street in front of what they called the "scab factory." There were many confrontations when non-union people crossed the picket line. Some were hurt even though there were police standing by to prevent these actions. As a result, the factory management was, many times, unable to conduct business for lack of labor. A neighbor who lived a block away from our Courtland Street house who was also a cutter came by one evening and asked me if I'd join him to work weekends in one of the scab shops. The owners were desperate and that made the pay very good. Being aware of the danger, I said "yes" and he promised not to tell my mother what we were doing. I got permission from the front office to take Saturdays off, my excuse being I had to take Mom to the doctor on Saturday. I told Mom I got a weekend job, not mentioning the scab shop, and had to be at work early. It was still dark this Saturday morning as we made our way through back alleys and climbing a fire escape to the third floor of the scab shop.

For more than a month it appeared we were not noticed and the money I earned made these scary weekends seem worth the chances I took. We were, of course, noticed, but Al, who was an important officer of the union, interceded saying to union officials he would take care of it. It was a Monday morning when Al during the usual 10 minute break sat down beside me and said he knew what I was doing these past weekends and suggested I stop. He would see to it that the union goons would back off. I took his advice.

Chapter 25

I was awakened about 2 AM by voices coming from downstairs. I started down the stairs and was greeted with cold air. The windows were open. The smell of gas was light, but still noticeable. Pop had attempted to commit suicide. They made an effort to speak quietly so as not to wake me. They were trying to hide the whole incident from me. Pop always had a strong will and he fought his illness above and beyond expectations, but I can see how the pain and desperation overpowered him. Since he wasn't even able to hold a pencil in his hand it had to have been a great ordeal for him to hang a blanket, closing the doorway between the dining room and the kitchen.

Mom knew something was wrong when she woke up, spoke to Pop and got no answer. She found Pop sitting at the table in the small kitchen with all the gas jets turned on. That morning Mom decided to stay home from work, hoping to comfort Pop. I didn't go to work either as I thought they both needed me. I went with Mom to Ben's Pharmacy to ask him for something stronger than the pain pills he was now taking. Ben, being sympathetic, had to refuse since Pop's prescription was only for a certain strength and the law didn't allow Ben to be generous. We were back again the next evening. I guess our depressed look was too much for Ben. He gave Mom something in a very small bottle saying only one every so often and for Mom to keep the bottle with her at all times. There was a little relief for Pop, but we knew it was only for a short time. Ben said he could not do this again.

Chapter 26

I was pleasantly surprised when Al Gerber approached me saying if I showed some effort to help the union by volunteering to do some union work, it would help towards getting me a union membership. Walking the picket line or carrying a sign, I thought, is little work for an opportunity like this.

It was Friday. Al asked me to meet him at 8th and Arch Street at 10 AM on Saturday. I arrived at the corner early, not wanting to miss this opportunity. Almost on time a car pulled up and from the back window Al called out to me to sit up front with the driver. As I got in I noticed Al in the back seat with two other men. The car turned down Arch Street. At about 4th Street the muffled sound from the back seat was a sound of agony. I turned to look at the disturbance as the man in the center between Al and the other man was tossed out of the car as we drove on. Al and his partner had broken the man's legs. The two window sash weights they used were on the seat where the victim sat. I felt myself getting sick and shouted to let me out of the car. We were near 2nd and Arch. Al told the driver to pull over and let me out. I didn't even look back as I ran all the way to Lit Brothers Department Store at 7th and Market, barely making it to the men's room to vomit. I had mentioned to Mom the night before that I was meeting Al so I expected her to ask what it was all about. "Al asked if I would do some picketing," I told her, "but I said no."

At our 10 minute break on Monday morning I asked Al why he needed me for this kind of union work. He said it wasn't his idea, but he had to go along with it. He said some union people thought I could be recruited. I let Al know that I didn't care to become a union member.

I may be over-anxious, but being blocked at every turn is discouraging.

Millions of people are still out of work in this industry and others and in every field the unions have instituted "closed shops." I just have to find a way to do better. $7 a week is all I'll ever get here at Lerner Blouse Company.

Chapter 27

Louie was head of the Pressing and Finishing Department at Lerner Blouse Company. For reasons unknown and unnoticed by me, he left his job months ago. He was so distant from our Cutting Department I never noticed that he was gone. Being close to the Sewing Department Mom knew him well. He lived around the corner from my grandmother's house. Many times when we visited and Louie knew we were at Grandmom's, he would drop by. Louie called one of the ladies in the Sewing Department that he knew to get a message to Mom. At home we didn't have a phone – one of the luxuries we had to forego. Louie made contact with a New York manufacturer and arranged to open a shop to contract their work. He wanted me to take charge of the Cutting Department. The shop would be in Quakertown, Pennsylvania, about 40 miles outside of Philadelphia. If I took the job it meant leaving Mom alone with Pop for five days of the week, but $40 a week was big money and a big opportunity for me. Mom saw the chance I had and, although I knew a part of her didn't want me to leave, she insisted I take the job. Pop showed his relief, thinking Mom would not work as hard as she did before. With a small advance Louie gave me, I had a phone installed and left a little money for Pop's pain pills and other little things he might need. Pop was a smoker. When he was still able and money was scarce, he would roll his cigarettes. It was his only vice. Whatever smoking did for him in his condition had to be a pleasant pastime. Those few minutes that does what it does for hooked smokers.

The Reading Railroad ran to those cities just north of Philadelphia going past Quakertown to Allentown then Bethlehem and a dozen or more towns beyond. I really just felt like a big shot. Sometimes I'd work Saturdays for the overtime money, but only till 2 o'clock to catch the train home. I decided some months later to buy a car. Since I didn't need it at work and to keep its cost down I would leave it at home so I'd have it when I got home on weekends. It was a luxury I felt would be good for all of us. We would go for rides and not too far places that we had never seen before. Mom, never forgetting she was a mother and had two other children, would sometimes say, "Let's visit Tillie or Sam." Their visits to see their mother and father were few. It's sometimes hard to believe the difficulties one had to find the 15 cents for car fare, but then I had the same difficulties not so long ago. I hoped their plight wasn't that severe and, if so, that would be their only reason for not visiting.

The New York parent company that helped create our contractor's shop was, of course, trying to evade the union. We heard that one shipment of finished dresses had found its way to the bottom of a mountain on its way back to New York. Although the long arm of the union was responsible, it could never be proven who was behind this and other despicable acts. I wasn't altogether anti-union. I would often see my mother and others toil so hard in hot airless rooms for their tiny $8 or $10 a week. If it weren't for the unions I'm sure they'd make less and work harder. The union's big battle cry always was, "Don't forget Triangle Waist." We were living at a time when very few people could afford to be independent.

The New York union had begun to do a real job on our parent company. They were hitting all their out-of-town contractors. We here at Quakertown were on their list. However, it wasn't necessary for them to confront us. The New York plant became a union shop so the rules agreed upon automatically closed down all non-union contractors shops. It wasn't a time for celebration, but we had a party at our shop to say goodbye to a group of new friends.

It was as though I should be home at this time. Pop developed a fever and complained about shortness of breath. I called the doctor and he suggested we put Pop in the hospital. We helped Pop to get in the car. My car was a Ford roadster with seating room for 2 up front and a rumble seat on the outside back of the car for two people. Of course, Pop sat up front with me and I helped Mom into the rumble seat. The doctor was already at the hospital when we arrived he directed the two nurses with him to get Pop into intensive care. Mom and I sat on the bench in the hall just outside the Intensive Care Unit. It seemed like forever until the doctor approached us.

"Pneumonia," he said. "He'll be taken to his room soon and you can see him then."

The oxygen tent covered Pop and a large portion of his bed. He couldn't talk, but raised his hand to assure us that he knew we were there. The doctor came in again and said he thought it best if we left in order to let Pop sleep. He gave Pop a strong shot to ease his pain and something to help him sleep. I don't know when Pop had the pleasure of sleep. We were back again the next day. Pop was awake, but still in the oxygen tent. He spoke to us in a very weak tone. We were almost unable to understand what he was saying. I asked him if he was being taken care of and he nodded. I had called Tillie and Sam the night before and they came to the hospital. What a family reunion this is! I'm sure seeing us all there sent Pop a discouraging message. Some hours later Tillie and Sam left the hospital and Mom and I went home. A call came that evening. Pop died. He was only 47 years old. Mom had been so used to this tragic life I think her first feeling was relief, more so for Pop than for herself. I picked Sam up the next day and we made the necessary funeral arrangements. Members of the family and friends came and went throughout the following week. With well wishers gone it was once again quiet in our house.

Chapter 28

I was very aware during the entire incident that I was unemployed. I scanned the newspaper's Want Ads and came across one for a Cutting Room Manager. The plant was in a town called Mau Chunk. I had to re-read the ad because of the town's name to make sure it was in this country. This was a ladies wear manufacturer in a coal country town somewhere in the coal region of Pennsylvania. I answered the ad by letter and the return letter stated approval. It would mean leaving Mom all alone and this time I was at grips with myself. Almost all shops in Philadelphia and New Jersey were union. I could not get a job here. It became a very difficult decision for me to make.

I had a week to decide and for most of the week I kept this job a secret from Mom. I finally told her and, like before, she insisted I take it. It was winter, more so in Mau Chunk since the town was in the mountains among the Appalachian chain. As I stepped off the train with the conductor's helping hand he warned me to be careful on the slippery slopes. I noticed too that I was the only passenger to leave the train. I asked the conductor for the center of town. He smiled like I may have been joking with him. "This is it," he said, "but if you walk up this hill you will have gone through the biggest part of town and you'll come to Main Street," he said pointing to a narrow path.

The town was two blocks long and the coal dust covered the snow making it look dirty. A grey pall hung over the mountain that loomed to the sky from the side of Main Street. I don't know at what elevation this is, but what looks like a cloud is hovering above my head I just might have been the only one to apply for this job. I saw myself as the hick from the big city. The street or path that led to the factory was a steep climb. Even as a young man I was puffing when I reached the front door of the factory. The owner, Mr. Cranopoulos, greeted me. He seemed angry or disturbed and took me on a tour of his plant. The cutting room was large, but I counted only five men. Mr. Cranopoulos explained what he thought were his problems in the cutting room. He, too, was a contractor for a New York firm.

The New York firm only had an office. Mr. Cranopoulos was their only source of labor. One thing was certain. The union couldn't touch him here. Salary was agreed to in our exchange of letters. I was pleased, but after looking around since leaving the train could see why I might have been the only applicant.

The hotel where I was to live looked like one you'd find out west during the time of Custer or Wild Bill Hickock. A walk up to the second floor, floorboards creaking as you walked. A wire hung from the ceiling in the center of the room with a light bulb at the end. A knob just above the light bulb turned it on and off. It was very difficult trying to find the knob in the dark. I never was one for luxury. If I wanted it here I would have a hard time finding it.

The men employed in the cutting room were the real problem. They came to work as they pleased; took long smoke breaks; sometimes not coming to work at all. There were these women, some of whom lived in my hotel. They were wives of coalmen. Their husbands would be in the mines for a week at a time since the mines were quite a distance from the only hotel in the area. I went to the hotel a number of times to get my cutters out of the ladies beds to come to work. It took only a month for me to quit.

Chapter 29

I convinced Mom to take a week off from work. We'd take a sort of vacation, not to go away, but just stay in the city to go to a movie and dinner and take a ride through Riverside Drive along the Schuykill River, go to lunch somewhere. She loved to take walks and we did a lot of that. It was during our vacation week that, just out of the blue, Mom wanted to visit Pop's only aunt and her son, Morris, his only living relatives. She was old and not too well and unable to attend the funeral service for Pop. Aunt Molly's son, Morris, greeted us at the door and Aunt Molly, in one of her best dresses, was sitting up in a chair smiling, saying she was so happy to see us. She had very few visitors and was unable in her condition to get around. On our way home Mom told me the story of how Morris gave up his life to take care of his mother. She was searching for another way to tell me how Morris might have found another way to lighten his burden so he would have a better life that he owed himself. I could see the difficulty we were having, searching for a better choice for Morris's benefit only to arrive at a decision that there was no other way.

Chapter 30

It was time again to look for work, but where? Some weeks went by and I was beginning to be angry with myself for seeing Mom go to work for me. I decided I would do anything and to hell with a future. I was two payments late on my car and I knew I'd lose it soon. I didn't care. Even menial jobs weren't available. My desperation must have shown when I walked in to see Mr. Becker of Milgrim Lingerie. A friend, Mr. Kaufman of Paramount Dress, wasn't able to hire me for anything, but gave me a recommendation for Mr. Becker. "The job of Sample Cutter is open" he said, "and if my present regular cutter doesn't return and you work out the job is yours." He took advantage of me salary wise, but I showed only gratitude. It was my first experience with ladies underwear, very fine fabrics, laces, etc. Mr. Becker showed me where I'd be working. It was late in the afternoon so he told me to report in the morning. Being hired in the capacity of "sample cutter" I was considered a Firm Executive and immune from union rules and regulations.

Off to the side and across the small room from my cutting table was Bertha. She would sew the samples I would cut. For the first week I was so engrossed in my new job I paid little attention to the arrangement of rooms in my corner of the factory. We were preparing for the coming season and the surroundings were hectic. It wasn't until the following week when it was "Show Time." In this corner of the factory and partitioned were three rooms in a row, all about the same size. The elevator opened to the Receptionist Station. The door to the first room off to the right led to the showroom. In preparation for the new season it was decorated nicely with a sofa, two upholstered chairs and the windows were draped and there was a bar off to the far wall that was fully stocked. It all stood on an Oriental rug. It looked like a very pretty living room. The doorway to the next room led to my cutting room. The doorway to the third room was the model's room. I'll always remember this Friday. Our sales people liked Fridays because the end of the week was a time when buyers started relaxing and getting in a festive mood. I couldn't help but notice the four models through the open doorway to the third room. Their room was well lit; the attendant ready to help them dress, undress and dress again. One at a time a model would pass by my table to enter the showroom. On their return they would start to undress before they reached their room in order to dress quickly for another style bra and panty. I was 19 years old, healthy and etc. Being obscured behind my table kept my embarrassment secret. Most buyers were men. I never could understand why. What an enjoyable and at times aggravating job. In bra sizes I learned about cup sized, A, B, C, D and WOW. The small raise I got after Show Time Week indicated that Mr. Becker was pleased with my work and my job was safe and steady.

Chapter 31

Like an illness that appeared terminal, the depression was the only concern people had. Making it till tomorrow was all that mattered. The newspapers and radio for I don't know how long, had been doing their job of keeping us informed of Nazi Germany's conquests. Many people here in the United States were concerned, but felt and thought the end had come when Hitler would say he wanted no more. I guess deafness and stupidity was another illness we had when Hitler would say and repeat many times, "Germany today, tomorrow the world." In the Jewish newspaper Mom would get from a neighbor from time to time was news often not found in our Philadelphia newspapers. Of course, the Jewish Forward was concerned about Jews and all other people who fell in the Nazi-dominating path. From whatever I have been able to read, the United States and the rest of the world kept taking a wait-and-see attitude while Germany bit by bit, swallowed up a little more of Europe. We always admired President Roosevelt and Mom had a plaster of Paris bust of him on the top of our refrigerator. It was a stain on the great reputation of this great president when he turned a ship full of Jewish refugees away from our country and their freedom. I would like to believe that President Roosevelt was coerced by people around him and not his personal decision that a boat load of Jews weren't worth the political risk. Maybe if it were two boat loads? Maybe 30 or 40 boat loads? Maybe let them all go down the drain to appease the hatred certain people have and who just hate who you are. What if Jesus had been on that boat? Who knows. People who oppose your religion will always find an answer to their hatred.

Chapter 32

I never had the money to join the guys to do the things they did. Many of them had two working parents. There were times I'd be invited to a house party and that kind of get-together was, for me, the best and we really had fun. A bag of potato chips or pretzels, some candies in a dish and sometimes little sandwiches made a little party very special. We would spin records and dance. Song sheets were a very big thing. Most times the girls would sing and the guys would just listen. Chaperoning was never necessary. Poverty kept most parents at home and many times they'd join us. Many of my friends were in or near my neighborhood and that helped to save carfare.

It was at one of the house parties that I met Ruth. She lived a few blocks from my house and several times we accidentally met at the local grocery store. I walked her home one time, carrying her grocery bag and nervously asked her for a date. She said, "Yes." I asked her if she liked football and again she said yes. It was winter, but being young and feeling it would be a nice day, I bought tickets for the Army/Navy game. I should have known that winter is no time for outdoor entertainment. It was very cold and it snowed, making for a terrible time. We left long before the game ended. On occasion I would drop by to say hi and Ruth would talk about some of her friends and things in general. Because of our last disaster I was almost afraid to ask for another date. I wasn't making that much money that I could date often. I still had to depend on our group get-together house parties.

It was Spring, the weather was warm on the day I stopped by to see Ruth. She was getting ready to go see a friend and invited me to join her. "Mitzie," she said, "lives on Rising Sun Avenue near Wyoming Avenue." I knew the neighborhood, having gone to the movie theater just down the street many times. It was only a 15 minute walk. Getting caught cleaning house wouldn't have bothered Mitzie if only Ruth had dropped in alone, but bringing me along unexpectedly, catching her disheveled and now flustered and everything else that would go with being surprised.

Mitzie was cleaning the piano. She was on the keys portion when we walked in, banging away with her cloth rag and trying to keep her head down to keep me from seeing her. "Sounds like Mozart," I said jokingly, trying to ease her feelings. "The piano sparkles," I said, still hoping the conversation will ease her discomfort. Ruth and Mitzie began discussing the things Ruth walked over for. I noticed Mitzie easing Ruth to the stairway and on up to her room, saying they would be back soon. They returned 15 minutes later. Mitzie's hair was combed and she was wearing a pretty blouse. The polite exchanges were made as we started to leave. I noticed Mitzie standing in the store entrance doorway watching us as we turned the corner. Ruth expressed feeling bad as if bringing me along wasn't the right thing to do. How would she know this was cleaning day?

Of course, Mitzie knew I had dated Ruth; after all they were very close friends and they must have shared some of their secrets. It was no secret that neither of us had serious intentions. I remember Ruth's sister saying intentionally or a slip of the tongue that her mother wanted Ruth to marry someone with money some day because she hadn't. Well, I guess that let me out.

Chapter 33

I walked in the house one evening from work to find Tillie and her daughter, Annett, visiting. It was a weekday and an unusual visiting time. Mom came right to the point. Mark, Tillie's husband, had lost his job a month ago and had so far been unable to find another. One word alone is not sufficient to describe Mark. He's a coarse individual, a slob. I have often seen him sit in the midst of company with his shirt unbuttoned and his belly hanging over his belt. He'd burp out loud as the urge approached. He was a very crude and common person, to a point where you couldn't have even a low key conversation about anything that concerned people or anything concerning everyday living. Tillie wasn't in that class, but I couldn't help feeling they deserved each other. Tillie said they were being evicted and had no place to go. They have a little money and promised to pay their own way if they could move in with us.

The second bomb to come was Tillie is pregnant.

I was silent for the longest time. I was thinking of Mom. She didn't need this disruption after the years of hell she lived through. I knew what it was like to have nowhere to go, but, damn it, some people deserve a break and some don't. Of course, there's Annett who was eight years old and soon there'll be another child. I guess we have to think of them. I looked at Mom and I could tell she was thinking of me, but also about Tillie's plight. She nodded silently, indicating yes. That's the way it went and there too went Mom's and my peaceful home.

Chapter 34

I still thought about Ruth even if I wasn't most welcome. It was easy to see that Ruth's father was not in charge. It looked like Mrs. Stoller was the strong one in that family and Papa Stoller took the easy way out, just not getting involved in the things that happened at home. The poor guy would have lost anyway had he ever wanted to voice his opinion about anything.

I was no great judge of girls. I think I knew five or six and of those I had been in their company for only a short time. I was in no position to get serious with anyone and it was the farthest thought from my mind. I wasn't out to find a girl friend. If someone very nice came along I don't know what I'd do. I called Mitzie and asked if I could come by. She said yes. We talked for awhile about me and Ruth. Mitzie already knew from Ruth that we had nothing going. I guess she wanted to hear how I felt. Mitzie wanted me to meet one of her other friends who lived just across the street. Rosie was another close friend so I'm sure she knows about my dating Ruth and also that we are just friends. I did most of the listening in our threesome conversation. Looking around while sitting with Mitzie and Rosie, it was obvious and sad to see how the depression had touched other people.

As we left to go back to Mitzie's house Rosie turned to Mitzie and said, "Bring him back again sometime." Mitzie began telling me about her family. "There are eight of us; four boys and four girls." At this point Catherine walked into the room and at once I was introduced. Catherine was the housekeeper to the family. Mitzie described the bigger house they came from before the depression and how Catherine came to them; how important she was helping to raise all the children. Mitzie's mother worked and that was the reason she was not at home at this time.

After losing his business, Mitzie's father was also driven by the depression to find another way to earn a living and became an electric appliance repairman. In the store out front and on the counters were many appliances to be fixed. I should mention, this was the Adams family. Before the depression, Mr. Adams had a men's habadasher's store and was the maker of the well-known "Adam's Hat." The depression robbed him of his livelihood like it did so many others.

Catherine wanted me to stay for dinner, but I felt so new I thought I still had not met any of the family. I had to decline. Besides, Mom was expecting me for dinner. I felt so pleased to be invited. From out of nowhere, scampering across the floor, came the family cat. "That was Sucker." Mitzie said and then she rattled the names of her brothers and sisters. I couldn't help thinking of the hardship that must exist here trying to stay alive. One thing in their favor was the fact that there were, unlike in my family, several people working. No matter how little they earned the small contributions had to help tremendously. I was so preoccupied with thinking of the Adams family I missed part of what Mitzie said, hearing only "oldest." Charles, then Rosaline, Dorothy, Arlin, myself (Mitzie), Jack, Teddy and Joan. There might have been a rule in this house and family – if a guy is entertaining a girl or a girl a guy the rest of the family will have to disappear. None of the kids were around or maybe they were too busy. I felt like staying longer, but I thought it best not to. As I walked through the store to leave, Mr. Adams was there and Mitzie introduced me. I walked home slowly, thinking about the short time I just spent with Mitzie. All I could think about was how good I felt being with her. Not quite the same as with Ruth.

As I opened my front door I was greeted with an argument Tillie was having with Mark. It was one of many we have heard since they moved in. When Tillie and Mark and Annett moved in we thought it only right that we all sit at the dining room table together for dinner, but these last months were too much. Mom never said a word and was constantly upset. Our house was small. We just couldn't call someone to the side for a private discussion without someone being near and overhearing. I wanted to spare Mom of having to listen to all this bickering and constant arguing. It couldn't be helped and I couldn't contain myself any longer. I got Tillie and Mark together. " I don't care if you chew each others heads off," I said, "but you can't do it here anymore. If you don't stop the fighting and be more considerate of Mom and me you'll have to leave. Don't make me get nasty too."

Mom and I often had our dinner in the kitchen. She tried to console me telling me many times not to worry about her; that Tillie's baby is due soon. It was the mother part Mom was using to soften me.

Mark wasn't pulling his part as he promised. I don't see how he could since he wasn't working. I'm sure Mom's slipping them some money only I'm not supposed to know.

It's a boy and there's no joy around the house. The bickering between Tillie and Mark has stopped. I guess out of fear of being kicked out, or perhaps it was Stanley, the new baby.

Chapter 35

Although the girls in Mitzie's group of friends were close she had one very special friend. It was on a Sunday afternoon. I only called Mitzie to say hello but she said if I wasn't doing anything would I like to take a walk. Among one of the many things the depression did for us, it made walkers out of us. Within the hour I was at the Adam's family house. Mitzie wanted me to meet her best friend. Just being with Mitzie I couldn't help feeling good.

Frances lived on C Street just four or five blocks from my house. I liked Frances almost immediately. Mr. and Mrs.. Dash, Frances' parents, were very pleasant and I found them enjoyable. On many later visits they would join us in our teenage shtick and would almost be like one of us.

Mitzie and I dated a few times, nothing special or expensive. We both seemed to enjoy each other's company. On a few occasions, because I felt so accepted, I would stop by without calling. I did so one time too many. I walked in on a date Mitzie had with someone else. Of course, I felt like a jerk. As I turned to leave I tried to dispel the look of a competitor by saying I just stopped by to show you something. Mitzie got up from her chair, walked towards me saying, "Call me." As I walked home I couldn't help but feel embarrassed. Then I thought, of course, she would know and date others. What if I'm turning out to be another brother. Am I being devoured by the green-eyed monster? I'm not supposed to get serious about anyone. I can't. I remember saying to my self I wouldn't know what to do if the right girl came along.

I could hardly wait to call Mitzie to apologize. She said she didn't mind, but calling first would be best. And then, like nothing ever happened, she started to tell me about Milton, her date. He and his family were in the luggage manufacturing business. I believe it was called "Belber Luggage." Anyway, Mitzie made it sound like only another date, nothing special. I looked at it as a challenge, a challenge I couldn't compete with. I just listened. When the conversation was over and we said goodbye I took a long hesitation and I'd better slow down. I don't know how much time went by. It was weeks I think and I wasn't feeling too good about it.

Chapter 36

It wasn't a "don't do it or die" rule, but girls didn't call boys. It was supposed to be improper. Hey! It was only a rule, not a law. So the call I got had Mitzie on the other end. Mitzie started, "I never mentioned it before about my group of friends. We're the Sub Deb Club." I came back with, "Sounds impressive." I'm finding myself being very careful with what I say. I don't know how I got it in my head after learning about Milton that I could be number two or three on Mitzie's list. I'm almost not fighting to be number one. Mitzie continued, "The Sub Deb Club is having a party and it's the girls who have to call the boys. Would you be my date?" "Yes," I said, so fast it must have had Mitzie looking at the phone. "The party will be in the basement of Ruthie Collins' house on Roosevelt Boulevard." Ruthie Collins was a new name for me to remember. I hadn't met her yet.

The basement was decorated with balloons and streamers. The walls were wood paneled. Around the perimeter of the room were chairs and off to one side a table with dishes of pretzels, potato chips, candy and cookies. It was their few pennies, saved for months, that enabled them to put on this very nice gathering. Almost everyone who was invited was there. Most of the people were unknown to me. I commented on the decorations when I was introduced to Ruthie Collins. Mitzie took me by the hand to the other side of the room to meet another good friend, Belle Aisen. After the hellos I said I knew a Max Aisen. "Oh, he's my cousin," Belle blurted, like she was glad we knew the same people. Between that and because Belle's father was a paperhanger like Pop was, we had something to talk about. At some parties I've been to after five minutes of introduction we would find ourselves sitting and staring at one another. I'm very relaxed here. The center of the room was open for dancing. I guess for the lack of a busier social life, I was not a good dancer. I should say not a dancer at all. The girls were good dancers and some of the guys who came all the way from South Philadelphia were also good dancers. I was satisfied to watch. Mitzie insisted on teaching me. As I moved clumsily around the room I hoped nobody was watching us. I just liked holding her hand.

Although Rosie was not serious about any particular boy, she did invite a favorite. She introduced Sid Doctor saying jokingly "He's really a cab driver." Rosie was delighted to be one of the hostesses and as the dishes of refreshments emptied she was to refill them. We'll never know what brought it on, but Rosie came out holding a box and one by one she tossed candy into the dish saying, "One farty candy here and one farty candy there." We all laughed, taking it as a joke, but Rosie was the only one not laughing. We'll never know why.

I walked Mitzie home when the party ended. I told her how glad I was that she called me and that I did enjoy the party and meeting the others in her "Sub Deb" club. Catherine was standing in the entrance to the store so she said with her Irish accent, "Catching a breath of air." We recounted things about the party for Catherine. For me it was the unexpected when Catherine turned to Mitzie and said, "When are you going to ask your gentleman friend to dinner?" Mitzie always said Catherine was a no nonsense person. How else could she endure raising eight children? Mitzie said, "I don't know. Maybe soon." It caught her off guard too, I guess, maybe more than it did me.

As I walked home I rehashed in my mind the whole day, especially the dinner invitation. In past discussions Mitzie would tell me that Catherine's approval or disapproval was the main and final stamp. I also thought about Milton. Milton lived in New Jersey and I wondered, would Mitzie have invited Milton instead of me if he didn't live so far away. I'm going to believe I won this date because she likes me better.

Chapter 37

In years past I bought fabrics for Mom for the clothes she made for herself and for others. I found most of the fabrics she wanted in a fabric shop in downtown Philadelphia. The name of the company was "Stapler." Mitzie had graduated from Olney High some months ago, but was unable to find a job. Without telling Mitzie I made an attempt to see Mr. Stapler. I missed him twice, but his son who worked at the store said there might be an opening. "The old man would have to do the hiring." I guess I was there at the right time. Mitzie came to the store with me for an interview and got the job. Her very first. In the weeks that followed I met Mitzie for lunch and a few times for dinner. The feeling of independence made her feel great.

It could be because of its beauty one of our special meeting places was the Art Museum on the Benjamin Franklin Parkway. One time we actually toured the museum. I wasn't really interested in art at the time.

Chapter 38

Tillie and Mark were screaming at one another again. Mom was sitting in a corner bearing the unpleasantness. I made the decision.

Mom said nothing, but I knew her well enough to read her face when I told her I was going to tell them to move out. I made a point by insisting they move out of the neighborhood. I'll make sure Mom doesn't become a baby sitter. The pall hanging over us was gone when they moved a week later and the look on Mom's face a little brighter.

Chapter 39

England's earlier appeasement overtures did nothing to diminish the fear and chances of all out war and conditions in Europe were having an effect on the United States. If you wanted to know more than the government was telling you had to read the Jewish Forward newspaper.

In the past our biggest enemy was the depression and it was hanging over us with no sign of it ending. With the fear of the chance we could become involved in this war as happened in World War I, we would find ourselves unprepared. President Roosevelt, even though he was not a military person, was clearly able to see the need for preparedness.

A lottery for choosing men to go into training for one year would be the system for recruiting. Local draft boards were set up to process the men for induction. They had the power to put men in classifications - if you were unfit physically you were, of course, not taken. Then there was the dependency classification. It all had Mom very upset. A better feeling if you want to look at it that way was that she was not alone. In the early drawings of this no lose lottery my number came up. At the draft board I was able to show a past history of my mother's dependency on me. They said they would take it under advisement. The letter that followed stated request denied since I had a brother and sister. Little did they know how they both added up to nothing. The only preparations I had to make were only for Mom. For what it was worth I called Tillie and Sam to tell them, if nothing else, look in on Mom as often as you can. The army hadn't changed the pay scale since World War I. It was still $21 a month. At the time of processing the paperwork I arranged for the money to be sent to Mom. I tried to spend the time I had before leaving with Mom, as the lonesome wait will be hard for her. My visit with Mitzie was short. We didn't talk much, but I said I'd write.

I don't remember if I kissed her. If I did, it was the first time.

Chapter 40

I knew I was headed for an experience I had only read about. We were shuttled from camp to camp. It appeared the mobilization was probably too big for our government to iron out all the first time problems to make mobilization and the system run smoothly.

While learning which foot was right and which was left we used sticks to substitute for guns. In one camp we lived in pup tents (2 in a tent). The second camp was an upgrade, a larger tent that held six men. Thirteen weeks of basic training was to prepare us for assignment to our parent home. We were divided in groups to be sent to different divisions. We may never see these same guys again. I was in a group that will be going to "2nd Division," Fort Sam Houston, Texas, Company I. Training was rough, even for career soldiers, some of which I found in my company. I was told by some old soldiers that the plan was to keep separate old friends, neighbors from your town, etc.

A career soldier in my company was an American Indian named Prince. Like with many others I would say hi whenever our paths crossed. He was in my squad so he was also in my barracks. The whole barracks this day was being punished for not passing the cleanliness check. Prince and a few other old timers were looking to blame some or any of the newer men, mainly because it kept them from going into town. Prince came over to my bed and asked to see my dog tags. On my dog tags was the letter "H" which stood for Hebrew. "You fuckin Jews are always getting us into trouble. I'm going to have to beat the shit out of you," he said. I had to look up at Prince's face. He was about 6 feet tall. He continued, "I hate Jews." I asked Prince to sit down on the bed next to mine. "Before we make any arrangements for this fight," I said, "I would like to try to understand some things I may have missed while I was growing up." Thoughts of Miss Gruber and fights I had as a kid in the 4th grade for being a Jew came to mind. I was hoping Prince would understand what I was about to say. "Some five hundred year ago or so people say Christians found this land. I would hope

95

you'd know the history of your people. I'm not an expert on your people's history, but I've read enough to learn what happened to your people." At this point a few other GIs overhearing our conversation, gathered around. "There were no Jews among these Christian soldiers/explorers and with the Cross of Christ as their symbol they came on your land and at their convenience slaughtered your people and took your land. The killing went on for centuries until your people were reduced to nothing as they are now. I would think that you would use and direct your energy toward trying to right this terrible wrong with those who made you a third class citizen and who still call you a fuckin' Indian. Now, as to our fight. I know, because of size, you can do what you just said you'd do. If it would end there I'd join you for this last time, but you hate Jews and at another time you would challenge me again. So with the guys around us here, to witness and understand that I mean what I say, I'll have to kill you."

The guys around our bed and Prince at first showed astonishment and for almost a minute there was silence then one GI said, "You're joking." I turned to Prince and said, "You decide if it's worth it." We all then continued to clean the barracks. There was no fight. Prince even tried to avoid me. "When Will It End."

I never had any money to join in a poker game. On our day off I'd just hang around camp. It was boring. On one Saturday I joined a bus load of guys to go into town to a party that was hosted by the City of San Antonio. There were a lot of girls at the party, but were hardly noticeable in the sea of GIs. I inched myself into a corner next to the coffee and doughnut counter. There wasn't too much room to move around so I stayed put. A girl with a hostess tag on her was right next to me pouring coffee and handing out doughnuts. During the lull moment since we were sort of captive, we talked. Her name was Allene. That was Mitzie's given first name. I remember Mitzie telling me that when she was born her father said she was as big as a mitt so she got stuck with the name "Mitzie." I said I had a friend back home with the same name. It helped start a conversation. After swapping stories for a half hour or more Allene asked if I was

96

busy tomorrow (Sunday.) I said I was the unbusiest guy in the Army. She said she would pick me up about 2 o'clock. Allene lived with her parents. I, coming from a big city was overwhelmed to see a banana tree in her yard. We spent the afternoon talking and looking through a family album. Allene's parents at times joined us in conversation. I was invited to stay for dinner. It was an unexpected pleasant day. Allene gave me her phone number and asked me to call her as it would be difficult for her to reach me so I said I would. I don't know if I should have, but in a letter to Mitzie I wrote about meeting and seeing Allene.

Chapter 41

Six months had passed and I was allowed a two week furlough. I was homesick and I knew Mom would be happy and anxious to see me so I borrowed money I needed from Uncle Sam to go home.

For Mom my being home, if only for a short time, was a tonic. Mitzie and her "Sub Deb" Club made a party and I was able to see some old friends again. Mitzie and I spent some time together, but I made most of my time available for Mom.

I noticed a small bottle of pills on Mom's dresser. She said it was nothing, just a minor problem. I didn't pursue it knowing it wouldn't help to probe anyway. The two weeks flew by and so it was back to camp. The next several months training was spent in the field. The field maneuvers were the toughest yet living in the open in all kinds of weather. I was called one day to our Field Command Post. My Company Commander handed me a paper from Red Cross Headquarters. Mom was very ill and it was advised I go home. My Company Commander intercede saying my year's service would be up by the time I would come back so he suggested and was able to finalize the papers necessary for my discharge.

From field maneuvers I was taken to Nashville for the train to Philadelphia. I would have liked calling Allene to say goodbye. I can still do it from home.

Mom knew when I'd be home and as I guessed she was in the kitchen whipping up one of my favorites. While wolfing down the medium rare calves liver and onions we talked about Mom. The pills kept her problem in check and the pills had to be near her at all times.

Chapter 42

Many industries have turned to defense work and many materials for private industry have become scarce. As a military veteran now and maybe with labor shortages I figured I'd have no problem with the union if I applied my skills at defense work. My status at this point is "Reserve." For their part in being patriotic an employer had to return to the veteran the job he held before going into the service. At Milgrim's Lingerie the shortage in fabrics was so great that my old job didn't exist anymore. They had been nice to me in the past; I wasn't going to make a case of it. Being a veteran now and seeing the swing to defense work I applied for work at the U.S. Marine Corps Quartermaster. I was put to work at once. My first job was sample cutting; almost like the job I had with Milgrim's Lingerie only not as pretty. When I got home that night I said to Mom, "We're going to move." On the coming Saturday we went out to look for a new home. The neighborhood of Logan was not too far from where we lived. It was much nicer than any we lived in before. It was a one-bedroom apartment on the second floor. I hesitated at first, but after speaking with the doctor, he, Mom and I agreed that if Mom wouldn't climb the stairs more than once a day it would do no damage. Mom said she had no reason to go down to the street anyway. On the following Saturday Mom and I went downtown to Gimbels Department Store. I bought all new furniture and a new rug for the living room. The studio couch in the living room would be my bed at night. Mom had stopped working long before I came home, but I was going to be sure now that she would never work again.

The move, the new furniture, my job and being home made a new person out of Mom.

Several weeks went by. I took Mom to the movies to see "The Good Earth." She and I had seen it twice before. The first time the theater was so crowded we stood in the back for the whole movie. The second time we sat, but for her it felt like a first time because she missed parts of the story the first time. So now for the third time she'll enjoy it again.

At home we talked about places I've been and of some of my experiences. She would only say, "I hope you will never have to use what you've learned." I began talking of some new fun things I was planning for us when Mom broke in, "Mitzie used to call often to see how I was doing. I think she's a very nice girl. She came with Frances several times to visit with me. have you seen her since you came home?" "Yes," I said. I knew what she was driving at so I said I would call her and plan to see her this weekend.

Chapter 43

I started dating Mitzie and liking her more on each date. We went to some nice restaurants, some movies and when we and the Sub Debs could all get together at the same time we had a little party. At Mitzie's house one early evening I met Mitzie's sister, Ro. We exchanged some small talk and Ro left for the evening. "Two of my brothers will be down in a few minutes," Mitzie said. "I mentioned you to them and they would like to meet you." As Jack walked in I got up to shake his hand. He said hello and that he was in some hurry, excused himself and left. "This is my oldest brother, Charles," Mitzie said as Charles walked in. As I shook his hand I looked again and said, "I know you. We met a few years ago." And Charles broke in, "Of course. North City Delicatessen." I came right back with "Chic," Charlie's nickname. "I guess the world is small as they say." Mitzie seemed more surprised than we were. Charles said he remembered stopping at North City Delicatessen with Max Asin and Joe Seebe when I worked there.

As Mitzie and I walked to Frances' house Mitzie said, "would you like to come to dinner this Friday?" I didn't even have to think about it and said yes.

It was a Friday to remember. At the table sat Mr. and Mrs.. Adams, Ted, Joan, Jack, Dorothy and Cousin Helen who, I was told, is a guest several times a week. Charles, Arlin and Ro had dates. Had they been available I don't know how we would all fit around the table. I almost forgot. There also were Mitzie and me. Catherine made the dinner and Mitzie and Dorothy helped serve. Catherine steered me to a chair and as she seated me said, "whoever sits in this chair (meaning boy) will marry one of the girls." (She had to mean Mitzie.) Mitzie in the kitchen heard Catherine and called out, "It's an old Irish grandmother's superstition so don't let it scare you." It was a noisy, but very nice evening. I thanked everyone for the invitation. We never had anything like this at my house or any house I've been to.

Mom waited for me to hear all about this evening and we talked till the early hours of the morning.

Chapter 44

I told Mom not to bag my lunch for a couple of days as I wanted to try the cafeteria at the Quartermaster. I thought, when I saw the crowd, that it meant the food was good; it would have been better if the line weren't so long and the waiting so long. There was hardly enough time to eat and get back to work. I did have a pleasant surprise though. In line, just a few people ahead, was Ro, Mitzie's sister. In all our conversations where Ro worked was never mentioned. I stuck my hand out and waved. Ro waved back and then came back to talk to me. She was new here, a good reason for not discussing it before. She was with some of her office people and needed some pointers so this time we couldn't sit together. We both said we would try again another lunch time.

I wanted to reciprocate for the parties that the Sub Deb Club gave in the past so, with some help from Mitzie and Frances, I was able to invite the right people and put together the right food and drink. On a date Mitzie and I had, Mitzie introduced me to cooked shrimp. It became one of my favorite foods. I took it upon myself to buy the shrimp for the party. I had no idea how much to buy for ten or twelve people that we had invited. I wound up having to fill the bathtub with ice to hold all the shrimp I bought. It wasn't meant to be, but became the idiomatic fun thing of the evening - Mitzie and her friends will never forget it.

Chapter 45

I was advised at work that I was being promoted. I was ushered into a room that was also an office with a desk, telephone and a coffee machine. I was to be a pattern maker, a better and more responsible job and, best of all, more money. All my past hardships seemed to fade away. I made a point this time to tell Mitzie the good news first. When I thought about it a couple of days later, I didn't mean to imply anything. I wouldn't, of course, mention it again. Mom, of course, was very happy. I wanted to do as much for her as I could. The raise I got came in handy. Mom wasn't feeling too well and seeing the doctor once or twice a month, plus medicine, was taking a big bite.

As far as I knew, Mitzie continued to date other fellows as I had hoped she would. In the back of my mind I always feared Milton. Frances casually mentioned once that Milton was still coming around. I'm 21 years old and with enough sense to remember that Mom still needs me, maybe more now than ever before.

An order from "Selective Service" was on the Colonel's desk calling me again into military service. "I do need you here," he said, "so I'm going to ask for a deferment for six months, the maximum time allowed." Such news for Mom isn't necessary for discussion so I'll keep it to myself.

Wanting to be with Mitzie was becoming a stronger will than I had power over. There was no other girl in my life and I was beginning to see how good a person she was. At the same time, my future began to look unsettled. I can't get myself to become committed and if I were bold enough to ask Mitzie to be my steady and she said no, who needs rejection and what would be different from the way things are? The only person I know who is in a hurry to see us together is Catherine.

Secret Number 1 has finally leaked. Ro was secretly married and she wants the family to know. For the family the news was received with joy.

Among Dorothy's dates was one fellow who was more persistent than most of Dorothy's other beaus and it wasn't too long after Ro's announcement that Dorothy became the family's number 2 bride.

The family knew that Chic had gone off and married some time ago. As an outsider I heard about it from casual conversation.

Of all the children, Arlin was pegged as the brightest. His scholarship to college was going to be interrupted by the draft. It was because of his reserved training that he was allowed to enlist with an officer's rank and it would also protect his scholarship. At its best, everyone's plans are being disrupted. In the following four or five weeks, whenever I spoke to Mitzie, plans for Arlin's wedding were being made. At this time, with war looming, I felt marriage didn't make any sense. The war in Europe was getting worse. We weren't being trained for nothing, and to go off for a year and maybe more if we're called to take part – I just don't see going off and leaving a wife to worry and wait.

At the Marine Corps Quartermaster it was easy to tell that mobilization was increasing because of the increase in uniforms that were being produced. It was becoming necessary for overtime work and signs of a second shift were showing. Colonel Bradford intervened once again when another call for me reached his desk. It was only for three months and the colonel said would be the last deferment.

I had no idea how I was going to prepare Mom for this again, but she was smarter than I was giving her credit for. Between her Forward newspaper and radio reports she knew as well as anyone that conditions all over the world were bad and her premonition of my status made it easier for her to accept the news about me.

The three months were like the blink of an eye. I found myself in the colonel's office for the finale. He said he tried again for a deferment extension, but was turned down. As he put it, someone outranked him. In the few days I still had at the corps the colonel said he'd be away and wanted to wish me well.

Chapter 46

It was a difficult goodbye at the apartment for Mom and for me. Mitzie was there too, telling Mom she would come to see her often, trying to help soften the agony. Mitzie went with me to the 30th Street railroad station. We didn't talk very much. At an arranged area in the station a large group of men had formed. They all held some small bag that I knew contained a few personal things given to them by the Red Cross. I had been through this area before. We said our goodbyes with Mitzie promising to visit Mom.

Chapter 47

Like once before, it was 13 weeks of basic training, much more up-to-date and more serious. I had a lot to think about, unlike the first time, so I kept to myself. I won't see any of these guys again at the end of 13 weeks and I see no need to make close friends. Again, I arranged to send my monthly pay which was a little more than the first time, to Mom. Again, I couldn't pal around with the guys nor did I want to. Howard's bed was next to mine. In the short time we got to know each other I found we had a lot in common. He was in a situation somewhat like mine. He too was sending his money home to his mother. We found ourselves alone many weekends, spending time at the enlisted men's club. Having been through this before I was able to tell Howard what we might expect. He seemed nervous most of the time, writing lots of letters. He said he didn't know too many people, but writing letters helped him pass the time. Most of them were to his mother even if he repeated himself.

Time sometimes seems to drag and other times it just flies by. It could be the thought of war breathing down our necks that's causing an unexplainable feeling.

I find myself thinking of Mitzie all of the time. From time to time I take my one-day pass to town just to get away from anything army.

I have no money, but walking around town taking in some of the sights gives my morale a little boost.

The music filling the street was coming from a shop down the avenue and as I approached the store front the large sign read, "Make your own recording to send home to Mom." I guess I was thinking more about sending a record to Mitzie – but what? The next three days were mine for the coal room detail – a job to keep the furnace going for the barracks. All alone in this small room I decided what I'd put on that record. I'll sing a song to Mitzie. Howard will lend me the money and in this coal room where no one can hear me (I think) I'll practice for the next three days I'm on this job. A favorite song of mine at the time was "Moonlight Becomes You." At first I felt awkward and silly belting out the tune while reading the words from a song sheet – and what if someone hears me - could they put me in the guardhouse for the disturbance?

It was Saturday and a store attendant led me into a glass enclosed booth. I was shown the switch for "on" and I could begin whenever I was ready. That awkward feeling was back and the pressure that I felt was reaching "explosion." I could feel the eyes of the people in the store watching me through the booth window. The playback to here my rendition and for me to rate my performance will be left to Mitzie.

We were already at war with Germany and with the bombing of Pearl Harbor we added Japan to our enemy list. Security became a very important matter for our country. I read of the necessity to intern most Japanese to minimize spying and possible terrorist disruption here in the United States. In discussing it with Howard we agreed it should also be done with people of German descent. It was obvious that the "German-American Bund" flew the American flag before them while paying allegiance to the swastika and to Hitler. The bund never hid the fact that they had what they called a fifth column operating in the United States. Almost at once I remembered talking to Pop about the bund some 14 years ago. Imagine how far back the Germans started to try to conquer the world. I thought about how strong hate can be to brainwash a people to do Hitler's bidding. With the sound of the word "hate" Miss Gruber came to my mind.

I was nine or ten years old and I recall an incident in our old neighborhood. Even though there was a school yard three or four blocks away from any direction, our group of boys who usually played together chose to play in some of the side streets and other special spots. One of the special spots was on Tabor Road, two blocks from our main street. It was on the grounds of a Proctor and Gamble factory. In the front of the building was a man-made mound. The building itself was set back quite a way from the street. The grassy mound was quite steep. It took, even for us kids, a lot of strength just to try to climb to the top. This mound was a great spot for us to play "King of the Hill." We'd choose sides and throw fingers to see who would be the defenders. The attacking force of three or four guys would try to reach the top of the mound while trying to avoid the thrust of the opposing group at the top. Most times the attacking group would be repelled and come tumbling down. No one ever got hurt and it turned out to be part of our everyday fun. Anyway, it was Saturday, late morning and we were playing "King of the Hill." (We weren't allowed to play here on a weekday when the factory was operating.) Off to the side we noticed people walking up a path that led to the rear of the factory building. No one paid any attention to them, but my eye caught a familiar face. Almost at the same time the familiar face was staring at me. It was Miss Gruber. I felt partially safe because it was Saturday. Pop knew what was behind the factory. In an adjoining building was the home in our part of Philadelphia of the German-American Bund. I was beginning to see the force behind Miss Gurber's hatred for me and, almost well hidden, the hatred for America.

Chapter 48

Because I had come this way once before Howard kept asking, "What's next?" The big difference this time was "war." An unexpected order one morning had us assembling on the camp parade grounds with duffel bag A and duffel bag B. We had dry runs before. It didn't take long before we learned that this was the real thing. As names were called we formed new lines, dragging our duffel bags. With the hot sun beating down we stood and sometimes sat for several hours. It was the "hurry up and wait" system at work again. When the trucks finally came we boarded and rolled off, not knowing where we were going. About one hour later we entered a very large area, almost as far as the eye could see. The trucks stopped, pulling up side by side, and then a shouted order to get out of the trucks. Directly in front of us was a railroad track and about the time everyone disembarked, the whistle of the oncoming train could be heard. An officer in charge of the train detail called out as he rode his jeep the length of the standing men to leave the B bag where we stood when we boarded the train. The A bag would stay with us wherever we went. It was hours before the train started for the prearranged destination. There was no way of knowing how long we were going to be on the train. It was several days later when we arrived at another very large area where trucks were already waiting for us. For the days we spent on the train many of the men, for comfort, removed their shoes. I did too. When the order came to prepare to leave the train I bent down to get my shoes, but they were gone. A dozen guys helped search the whole car with no success. I don't know why, but from day one when I entered the Army, I kept my civilian slip-on shoes and they were in my A bag. Of course, I put them on.

As we got off the train we immediately lined up for a head check. An officer walked through our lines as we counted and as he listened he made an eye check on the way. His eye caught my shoes. He stopped, looked down and shook his head and walked on without a word. It was almost comical. As we climbed into our assigned truck one of our group asked the driver where we were going. "Don't know," he answered. He did know, but was ordered not to tell for security purposes. Our trip was comparatively shorter than others we had taken. We entered what we thought was to be our new home only to be advised by our driver when we stopped that this was Camp Shanks. We all knew Camp Shanks was the last U.S. stop before going overseas, either the European Theater as it was called or the Pacific. The choice was made for us.

We stood in front of a row of barracks where the trucks dumped us and left. We were shown our barracks and told if we're here long enough we'd be sleeping on the mattress only. An additional order was to keep our clothes on at all times. I dropped my A bag on my bed and, looking at my watch, saw that it was 9 AM and Camp Shanks was in New York and New York was only a couple, or at most, three hours from Philadelphia. I gave birth to an idea. A pass for a day or maybe two! I found the orderly room and I noticed as I walked in a captain and two sergeants. Saluting, I said, "Sir, could I get a pass?" They all laughed. "Do you know where the hell you are?," the captain said. "Yes," I said. "I live in Philadelphia, a couple of hours from here, so I thought..." I didn't get a chance to finish. "No passes from here," the captain said. For what seemed like a lengthy silence as I stood there, one of the sergeants said to the captain, "Go ahead, give him a pass." The captain hesitated, but then, lifting the desk blotter, pulled a pass from among other papers. As he signed it he said, "this pass is good only until 6 AM tomorrow morning. If you're not here it's my ass and if it's my ass, it will be your ass." I suddenly froze. "What the hell now?" the captain said. "I have no money." I said. The silence was shattering for the longest time. As I started to return the pass one of the sergeants who had said nothing since I entered the office pulled a bill from his pocket saying, "I came out way ahead in poker last night," as he handed it to me. "Only till tomorrow," I said. I thanked them all, saluted the captain and walked out. Without even looking I crumpled the money in my fist and shoved it in my pocket. I ran to the camp entrance where I caught an army bus headed for town. I asked the driver to direct me to the train station, telling him at the same time that I had an overnight pass. "Hold onto you're A bag," he said. "I'll take you right to it." I was too excited to think, but I was guessing the bus driver was violating a bunch of rules. As I nervously sat up front near the driver I felt the bill in my pocket. It was $10. When I get back I'll give him a $20 for it," I said to myself. "This all seems unreal." It was happening, but I couldn't believe it was happening to me.

It was Saturday. I hoped Mitzie would be home so while waiting for the train I called to let her know about my pass and for her to call Mom to let her know I'd be there soon. I also checked the schedule for my return. It was Sunday at 3 AM and would be no problem getting back in time.

It was a hectic visit, running from Mitzie's house to see Mom and back again to Mitzie's house, stopping to see Frances and Rosie on the way.

I decided to tell Mom where I was headed because from here on the mail would not be as often and I knew that would frighten her just as much. She showed no expression, maybe to make me feel like she was stronger than I knew her to be. I wasn't fooled, but made no more of it. Mom kept saying, "Don't be late getting back."

There was so much I wanted to say to Mitzie. The words wouldn't come. My mind was being numbed anticipating the little time that was left. I looked at my watch for the umpteenth time as it was getting late and early Sunday morning city transportation is few and far between. Mitzie wanted to join me to go to the station. I wanted to be with her every minute so I agreed. It was getting close to 3 o'clock and we kept saying trains are usually late. No need to worry. The subway stopped at the North Philadelphia Station and we thought it best to run. Up, up, I don't know how many steps to the train platform, reaching it in time to see the back of the last car of my train leaving the station. I scanned the schedule on the board while I felt a cold sweat. The next train was at 5:20. I'm going to be AWOL. Mitzie was calm so when she said you'll just explain what happened. They'll understand. I accepted her logic and said, "I hope you're right." Mitzie insisted on staying with me

117

till the next train arrived.

We talked a lot of everyday things. The station was just a passenger pickup. It didn't have facilities for coffee or anything like that.

The 5:20 was right on time. The minute it took for the "all board" was a silent one. I kissed Mitzie like a brother might, not like I knew I loved her. I wish I had the guts to say it. I spent the whole hour and a half it took between cities trying to figure out what to do when I got to camp and how to go about it. I just knew that if the army goes by the book I could be headed for the guardhouse and then some. Upon arrival at Grand Central Station there were MPs patrolling. (How does one walk without attracting attention?) One of many signs pointed the way to a waiting bus to Camp Shanks. From a short distance I could see an MP checking passes at the door of the bus. "I'm a dead duck now."

It felt like it came out loud as I talked to myself. With my eye on the bus I noticed that the MP was called away. I hurried my pace and got on the bus. The driver said, "Snap it up, I'm late." and took off. I knew the MPs at the gate would check me so I asked the driver to let me off a little before the main gate. I bet he sensed I was in trouble when he said, "My regular stop is at the gate but okay." I decided to take a side road that looked like it skirted the camp grounds. As I walked I thought if a sentry challenges me I don't know what today's password is. I wasn't familiar with the area, but a mile or so down the road I could still see the barracks in the distance off to my left. At that point, not seeing a sentry, I climbed the barbed wire fence, painfully. I started walking toward the barracks, feeling only half safe. Suddenly I looked around me. I was standing in the middle of the parade ground, much of Camp Shanks in my sight, and there wasn't a single person to be seen. I stood there, all alone. A scary feeling like I had never experienced before in my life. I couldn't be in the wrong camp. Even the bus destination said Camp Shanks. Now to find the barracks I was assigned to. From this point of view they all looked alike. It never dawned on me to learn the name of the street my barracks was on. I knew now I had to report in and would have to confront someone

118

in charge (officer of the day or whatever the system is here). I finally found the orderly room where I got my pass. A captain sat at the desk, not the one who gave me the pass. I saluted and handed my pass to him. He looked at the pass and looked at me and with a tone in his voice like he'd done this many times before, he said, "I'll have to make a report. What should I write on it?" I started to tell an almost believable story about missing the train because it came in early and that I missed it by one or two minutes. "I'm only about five hours late reporting, sir." He wrote as I talked then turned his report to face me for me to sign. He asked me if I had been stopped by MPs. I didn't want him to know how I tried to dodge them and I just told him no.

As the captain put my report in a file jacket he turned to me and said, "the guys that were here left at 2 AM this morning for the Pacific." I didn't know what to think or how to feel. On the way to my barracks I passed the mess hall. It was just about noon so I joined a few others in line for lunch. I knew now my barracks was just down the street and there on my bed where I threw it was my A bag.

Chapter 49

The feeling is indescribable, being in such a giant military city virtually alone. The last time I slept was three nights or days ago with only a few minutes of shuteye on the train. How lucky can I get with all this quiet. I unrolled the mattress and was asleep before I had a chance to think. A motorcycle speeding past the barracks woke me up. It was almost 6 PM and my first thought was chow. I wasn't fully awake so I went out to the front step and sat down rubbing the sleep out of my eyes. The stillness filling the air had an eerie feeling. The captain from the orderly room drove by and my first thought was, "He's now going to put me under arrest." "Chow will be at 8 o'clock," he said, and drove on. Eight o'clock was generally late for chow, but I guess because of the nature of the camp, the time for things in this place is different.

In this stillness while sitting on the top step I heard a rumble. I looked at my watch and saw that it was almost 7 o'clock. The rumble was the first of a convoy of trucks that began to pour into and onto the parade grounds right in front of me. Truck after truck, falling in side by side only 50 feet from my top step and the pouring of men from the bowels of these trucks continued for almost an hour. Thousands of men formed lines standing in the settling dust kicked up by the trucks. This is the most stupendous sight anyone could ever experience. I had a front row seat. I began to understand the 8 o'clock chow time.

In another part of Camp Shanks I learned a similar operation was going on. Unlike another similar experience, the trucks remained in place. Orders were being barked at the new arrivals to eat and return to the same spot where they were now standing. I went with them to eat. We all returned as ordered, they to their standing spot and me to the top step of the barracks. It was close to 10 o'clock when an officer brought the men in the field to attention. They're being told that tags will be given to them to be tied to their front jacket button. The tag will have a number and a large letter like A or B and your group leader will explain their purpose. I began to feel that by some snafu I was forgotten and this top step is to be my home for the duration. An officer approached me, handing me a sheet of paper that turned out to be a roster and a handful of tags, saying "You're in charge of 100 men." He didn't even wait for my salute, but turned and left. I didn't waste any time getting to the orderly room. The same officer of the day I had met before was at his desk. "Sir, I'm only a private. There must be some mistake putting me in charge of 100 men." "No mistake," he said. "Your file shows you have had more training than these men so that's the reason you were put in charge. Read the orders that came with the roster and explain the contents to your group." As I walked back to the men still standing in the field in front of my barracks I said to myself," "I guess I'm going too, and nothing more will be done about my being AWOL."

The tags with the large letter "B" were meant to identify my group while the letter "A" would identify the hammock area that the group would sleep in while on the ship.

I counted off 100 men, giving each one a tag as I counted and, not having any other orders, I told them they could go into the barracks to sleep if they wanted to. It was midnight now and the air was filled with anxiety. How could anyone sleep feeling the uncertainty of the future. For myself, I only had about five hours sleep in almost as many days. Maybe I'll sleep tonight. I unrolled my mattress and plopped down.

I lay on my bed thinking about the spectacle I had witnessed. I knew I was part of a similar show only a few days ago, but tonight I had a different view and it was powerful. I remember the captain saying as he was explaining my job that 18,000 men were unloaded here tonight.

Chapter 50

Whistles are blowing and there's shouting. Is this another one of those horrible dreams? I looked at my watch and it read 2 o'clock. It was 1:30 when I lay down. The shouter returned calling out, "Roll up your mattress and, leaders, assemble your groups outside."

After the head count and in an orderly manner we headed for the trucks, filling them as we filed by. After a minute or so in the truck I started acting like a leader should. I pointed to one GI telling him to help me keep all those in our group with the letter "B" together. The number 4 on the tag meant "Hold Number 4" on the ship.

From Camp Shanks to the dock was a comparatively short haul. With the police escort there was no stopping, not even a slow down. The second we arrived the order was given to board the ship and we waited our turn. Hold Number 4 was a crowded and depressing sight. (It should have been named "hole" number 4.)

Again the army had it all figured out. Only 50 hammocks for 100 men. Lucky that I went to school long enough to know that meant the men would have to sleep in shifts. I pointed out to the men that while one slept in the hammock another guy could sleep on the floor if he didn't mind the hardness. I suggested numbering tags 1 to 50 and that group could sleep first. I did not include myself in the group. Not giving it a thought before, I didn't have a tag for myself. I didn't know what I was going to do for myself. I asked if anyone was sick and half a dozen guys raised their hands. Lucky for them they were joking. I wasn't joking when I said, "Sick call will be in the morning. I'll be here to take your names." I sought out the infirmary some four or five flights up. Signs and arrows marked and pointed to the pill dispensers. Signs and arrows also pointed to the mess hall. They won't need a leader to find it.

Having lost track of time getting the men settled and being inside the bowels of the ship I didn't realize that whole day had gone by.

With the little sleep I had I wasn't feeling that good myself. I dragged myself and my bag up to A deck. The fresh air, if that's what it was, was a lot better than in Hold No. 4.

We must have been the first to board ship. No one except for British crew people were on deck. I dropped my bag along side the rail using it as a head and back rest and fell asleep. It was dark and very late into the night when I awoke. I don't know how long I slept, but my first thought was about my men in Hold No. 4. I found them. A few guys said everything was all right so far under the circumstances. No one was sick and I was assured that it wasn't necessary for me to look in on them. They had found the way to sick call and the mess hall and so far no disagreements over the sleeping arrangements. They realized this was also the first time for me. When I mentioned I hadn't eaten for hours one of the guys threw me an apple. He said there were a million of them in a bin in the mess hall. I took myself and my apple back to my bag on A deck. It was difficult to see anything looking over the rail. Large ships on either side obstructed the view. I walked down the length of A deck and found to my surprise that we were on the Queen Mary.

It was a day or two or three since we boarded and the ship was beginning to show signs of crowding. I went down to look at the mess hall. The main lounge had been converted into one big dining room. Rows of crude tables and benches and two long chow lines (serving line) met from two sides of the redesigned lounge. The lines never ended. Breakfast ran into lunch and lunch ran into dinner. I couldn't buck the line nor could I find where it ended. I picked up another apple and went back to A deck. The few times I walked A deck I did notice some of the rooms just off the walkway. Once in awhile I would see a British person who obviously worked on the ship. I was either very bored or still very tired from the past seven or eight days. Again, I crouched down against the rail and leaning against my bag, I fell asleep. It was the fourth or fifth day of troops boarding the ship. The traffic on A deck increased considerably during the hours I was asleep. All I could see milling around A deck were officers. I sat on my bag, leaning against the rail, trying to decide if I should find a place in the chow line or settle for another apple.

An officer approached me. I stood up and saluted. He was a colonel and he wasn't smiling. He was a little gruff when he spoke. "A deck Is designated for officers only and I expect to see you gone in the next few minutes." I saw nothing wrong with my being there in an out-of-the-way spot, but he must have felt that my being there would tarnish the brass. He left and in a few seconds was out of sight. I bent down to grasp my bag to throw it over my shoulder and as I did another officer, a major, was standing next to me. I dropped my bag and saluted. The sound of his voice was pleasant. "I noticed you sleeping here since yesterday," he said, "and I heard the colonel ordering you to leave. I knew something like this was bound to happen as it was only a matter of time." He continued, "See that room over there?," pointing to a door with a brass A12 on the head. "It is reserved for a colonel from my outfit. He may or may not be joining us. If he's not here by midnight, take that room." I saluted saying thank you. I moved to the other side of the ship and slipped down along side of a bin that stored life preservers. From either end of this walkway I was well hidden. I waited till a little past midnight to be sure. I tried the door knob. The door opened and the room was unoccupied. No sooner than I shut the door behind me when a knock on the door gave me a horrible chill. I thought I was being watched all along. I opened the door and there, with his British accent and with a tray in his hand, he said, "I'm your Steward, Sir." As I took the tray, too astonished to say anything, he continued. "You may ring me any time day or night for anything you want." He pointed to a button near the bed. He saluted while announcing that breakfast would be at 8 AM. Of course, I must still be dreaming. I was once told it comes from being exhausted, not enough sleep, etc. I was wrong. The little sandwiches were real. I don't know what was in them and I didn't care. The few cookies that were also on the tray added to this unexpected treat.

The room was small. There were no windows or a port hole. With the door shut and the light turned off the room was pitch dark. The white sheets on the bed were as much a treat as the tray of food. There was nothing left to do but go to sleep. I was getting into bed when there was another knock on the door. Oh, I thought. This time I'm caught and they're here with handcuffs. I opened the door and it was the steward with a tray of fruit. I lay on my soft mattress bed thinking how important the colonel that was supposed to be here was. Imagine, going to war first class on the Queen Mary. It must have taken only seconds – I was asleep. I might have slept forever were it not for the knock on the door. It was the steward with breakfast and as I opened the door I noticed it was daylight and more frightening, we had moved out. We were at sea. The steward said we left the harbor about 2 AM. For breakfast I had some kind of fish, scrambled eggs, a dry roll and coffee. I decided, for safety sake, I'd keep the door locked at all times. When the steward came for the dish and tray I told him I would ring when I wanted something and if he brought me something for him to knock only once. I would forego all the special service and I would check on the men in Hold No. 4 at night. With the ordered "blackout" it was impossible to see anyone or anything at night. Only once during the day I managed to get to Hold No. 4 undetected.

We zigzagged for four days and on a misty morning we docked in Glasgow, Scotland. With all of the confusion nobody saw me leave my room. I joined my group in Hold No. 4. As we assembled on the dock, other assigned officers took over. I was no longer a leader. I was again just one of the GIs.

On the road about 100 yards from the dock a convoy of trucks was already lined up to take us to I don't know where. The move was a new experience for most of us, being in this part of the world, to still be in daylight at midnight when we reached our destination. We had arrived in a city somewhere in England.

Our convoy was made up of men with tags A, B, C, D, etc. Another use of the system other than for sleeping on the ship. The 18,000 or more men from the ship were divided into groups to be taken to a number of other areas. Not everyone in our group was billeted the same way. I found myself in a house with five or six other men I didn't know. The row houses on both sides of our street looked the same and there must have been many of them to accommodate our group alone. We weren't allowed to wander for the time we were here because, not too far off was a community of civilians. I learned we were in the city of Birmingham, England. Our stay here was to be for one or two days as we were being assigned to our parent division and from here to our next home. My assignment was to join the 11th Infantry of the 5th Infantry Division, also identified as the Red Diamond Division. Again, waiting trucks stood by to take us to another new home near a town called Andover.

The 5th Division had been stationed for some past months in Reykjavik, Iceland and we were now going to be in a British camp called "Tidworth Barracks." Early the next morning we loaded ourselves on the trucks and bounced along for most of the day on our way to our new home.

All these guys are new to me. Making new friends seems like a gigantic chore. They probably feel the same. In the bunk next to mine lived this big fellow. A 6′ tall person with very broad shoulders and very large hands. Because of his massiveness he stood out prominently. "I'm Martin," I said, holding out my hand. "I'm Stanley." As big as he was that's how pleasant he sounded. We exchanged small talk, learning a little more about each other. When he talked about people in his family from their names alone I guessed he was Polish. "Yes," he said at one point. "I'm Polish." I wondered to myself how many Jew haters out there would try to goad Stanley into some confrontation with a stupid Polish joke or by just saying "I hate Pollacks." Stanley's last name was almost impossible to pronounce. We all addressed one another by our last name so, with Stanley's permission of course, he accepted the name, Polsky, which was given endearingly. Polsky and another guy in our squad, a regular called Meathead, and I became friends.

Chapter 51

For five or six weeks I have taken part in all training exercises, still wearing my civilian slip-on dress shoes. The soles even when new were rather thin and now they were almost worn out. Several attempts were made in the past to get a pair of GI issue shoes. Having been so detached from a regular outfit since the end of basic training, there just wasn't a quartermaster depot within our reach. Orders on the company bulletin board called for a 20-mile hike in the morning, part of which would include a forced march. During my one year stint before, I took part in many such hikes and I would have gone on this one too if I had shoes that supported my feet enough to take me through from beginning to end. It wasn't my decision to make. The authority to go on a hike or not would have to come from the company medics. At 7:30 AM when it was sick call time, I joined eight or ten other GIs. Colonel Becker at the infirmary was furious when he saw the shoes I was wearing and training in. He just wrote on my sick call report, "Excused from all training activities until Private Tucker can be fitted properly with shoes." He then asked me to explain the civilian shoes. "Sir," I said, "I did have a second pair of shoes in my B bag. When I gave up my B bag at Camp Shanks prior to shipping out it was put on a ship destined for the Pacific. I didn't get to go to that theater." (I didn't want to make a long story about missing the train and being AWOL and as a result being separated from my B bag.) About the time I got back to my barracks nearly all the guys were outside lined up and prepared for the long hike. Captain Carl, our Company Commander, was in the barracks making sure everyone goes. We were, at this point, alone, and I handed him the report from sick call. His face turned red and it looked like he was going to tear up the report. Shouting quite loudly he said, 'You fuckin' Jews are always trying to get out of doing anything you don't like." Now I was outraged. The report came from an officer outranking the captain and one he must honor. Anyway, his remark was uncalled for. If he weren't an officer I believe I would have torn into him disregarding the consequence. I tried to compose myself and said, "Sir, I'm at a disadvantage. If I beat the hell out of you I go to prison. If you beat me you go to jail, maybe for the rest of your life. If you're a man and not a shit head you will go to headquarters now with me and make your complaint to the colonel." The captain, knowing he was wrong and also aware of the consequences he would face, threw the report to the floor and stormed out. I sat on my bed for an hour trying to figure out what had just taken place. If it were a soldier of Polish extraction in my place he would have said, "all you fuckin' Pollacks" or if Irish, would he have said, "all you fuckin' Micks" or an Italian, would he have said, "all you fuckin' Wops." What kind of Christian is he? What will it take for people like this to become decent human beings? I walked to the doorway of my barracks and stood looking up and down the company street. It's going to be a long day. I missed my breakfast just to get to the medics. I have never been on sick call before and wasn't sure of the procedure. I walked through the mess hall thinking I could get a cup of coffee. I could hear the noise from the kitchen, a combination of KPs cleaning up and others even though it was morning, preparing for dinner. The company won't be back till then. "Hi, anybody home," I called out. And with that the mess sergeant stepped into the doorway. We stared at one another for a full minute before I said in a questionable tone, "Max Aisen?" He returned with "Marty?" Shaking hands and a slap on the arm and Max called to someone in the kitchen to come out and meet an old friend. When I asked if I could get a cup of coffee, Max said, 'I have something better." About 20 minutes later the something better was a big steak. We talked, of course, about North City Delicatessen, how I met Chic Adams again and how I got here. I told Max about this morning's incident. Max concurred that Captain Carl was a no-good S.O.B., but, luckily for Max, he didn't interfere too much with him or the kitchen. When I told Max of not seeing him the many times I sat and ate here, Max said he had been on a two week pass and a couple of weeks at school learning what to do in different situations in combat.

Max had things to do so I left and went back to my bunk. At its best, I thought, life with Captain Carl was going to be hell. I would get every rotten detail. I'd be put in some very dangerous positions on maneuvers and I'd be confined to barracks on trumped up charges. I knew he could make me wish I could disappear. The word "disappear" struck me like a musical chord. I hopped up and was off to headquarters. A sergeant interviewed me while checking off certain things on a form. "You can only get a transfer within the division," he said. I told him I'd be back after I thought about what I'd swap. As I walked slowly down the street, the next building had a sign over the door. Provost Marshal. MP, I thought. It won't hurt to inquire. Captain Couty asked me to sit down after I saluted, and addressed me. His voice was pleasant. I told the Captain about the incident with Captain Carl. Captain Couty understood quite well when I said it would be a bad choice to stay with the 11th. Captain Couty made some notes as I spoke. He then said, "Get your things from your barracks and come back here. Don't talk to anyone." On my return I was assigned to an MP squad and Captain Couty, taking my M1 rifle, handed me a Thompson sub-machine gun, better identified by most people as a tommy gun. I used the tommy gun before in basic training as I'm sure my record shows, but I couldn't help feeling like a one-man fortress. The First Sergeant took over when the captain dismissed me. First Sergeant Evans was a stone-faced looking guy. I'm sure he got to his post the hard way. In the army you have to earn your rank. Sergeant Evans was a regular army soldier. "When you get to know me," he said, "you'll be calling me Pappy like the rest of the men so if you want to, you can start now." Sergeant Evans showed me to my barracks. The upper of this bunk bed he said had to be my only choice since "Pig" was living in the lower. (I'll explain abut Pig later.) My duties were very different. Most important, it appeared I'd be a lot better off here. I just wondered, could Captain Carl be looking for me?

The next day Sergeant Evans told me to try the Quartermaster for shoes. The only thing they had were paratrooper boots in my size. I was also resupplied with all the things I had in my lost B bag. With my new clothes, boots and my tommy gun slung over my shoulder I looked like an "Uncle Sam Needs You" poster. In the weeks that followed I put a lot of effort in my duties. I wanted to show Captain Couty I would not let him down.

Chapter 52

Tidworth Barracks was not to be our base as being moved around looked like something the army liked to do. Once again we loaded ourselves into trucks in an early morning order (the army has a thing against sleeping) and late in the afternoon we found ourselves facing the English Channel. The troop ship, Santa Paula, docked in the harbor was waiting for us. The ship appeared too small for a division of men and it was. We crammed ourselves into any space we could find.

Where we stood we were almost shoulder to shoulder and where we sat we were almost on top of one another. The bitching simmered down when we learned the trip was short. We were headed across the English Channel to Northern Ireland. Our ship anchored off shore and landing craft waiting for us shuttled us to the small town of New Castle.

New Castle was set in a valley in the shadow of the grey, brown Mourn Mountains. When the entire MP company landed we formed a double file and walked the mile and a half to our bivouac area. From the road and looking down into a valley was a set of Quonset huts and jutting into the air among hundreds of trees was the real ancient, 400-year old castle of New Castle. It was to serve as division headquarters.

From the top of the hill I could see the Quonset building where we would live. It, along with the others, looked like the half of a gigantic sewer pipe. It was the first building of "A" Group as we entered the valley. Entering our hut, I got the feeling others lived here before. Nothing looked new. The bunks were crudely made of wood, like they were roughly cut from the tree and nailed together, maybe hurriedly.

The mattress was made of burlap, a large bag stuffed with straw. The designer of this furniture piece didn't have comfort in mind, or maybe it was purposely designed for discomfort. The pot belly stove stood on a dirt floor, as did the bunk beds. Light coming from the three windows didn't diminish the dismal look. If for no other purpose, we should learn to appreciate the things we will enjoy when we return to a better life.

Chapter 53

It was only a week since we settled in New Castle camp when Captain Couty called me to his office. "I see by your record," he said, "that you have been in the service almost a year and never had a furlough. It won't look good for me if this goes any further and a little break for you won't hurt either." My first thought was that here sat a man who took time to know the men in his command and has shown he was a caring person. "Sir," I said, "I can't take a furlough. I have no money and if I did, where would I go? I have arranged to have my money sent home." "I see that in your file," he said, "but I can arrange for you to borrow against your pay with the smallest pay-back amount." "I suppose," I said, " I could go to England. There might be more to see and more to do there." Captain Couty agreed and said that a boat to Birmingham from Belfast leaves on Wednesday about midnight and I could catch a ride to Belfast from camp. I was going on furlough, but the will to go just wasn't there.

The boat was small. It carried supplies from England to Ireland and back again. There were no passenger accommodations and the only place to sit was on a hard bench in a very small area that was supposed to be a lounge. Because of the war, like other means of transportation, the boats were never on time, probably a security measure. The channel was rough. We bounced like a cork in an electric mixer. Two British WAFs commandeered the only bench so I decided to go up on deck. It was so dark I couldn't see my hand held in front of my face. We had been out about a half hour when the sound of a cannon fire came from the bow of the boat. I inched my way, holding onto anything I could, towards the bow. The man behind the cannon at the tip of the bow knew I was there even though he couldn't see me. "What's happening?" I asked. He answered, "Shooting mines out of the water." The sailor manning the cannon laughed when I said to him, "And I'm supposed to be on vacation."

We got to Birmingham safely and my first move was to locate a Red Cross station. They helped put me up and suggested where I could go for food since food was a scarce item in all of England. I really didn't have enough money to go traveling around the country and wherever I went everything was so bleak and dreary.

Birmingham was an industrial city geared only for war work. It wasn't a fun place. There were no service clubs for off duty military people, be they American or British. I couldn't take any more so after five days of my two week furlough I dared to cross the channel again and returned to camp.

Captain Couty understood my dilemma. I never thought I'd be so glad to see the army again.

Chapter 54

I'm beginning to know most of the men in our company. It's easy to pick out the other two Jewish guys in our company. Sol Agnes from New York with his accent and actions really advertises the city he comes from. In New York he'd just melt into the crowd. The other was Sidney Witter from Chicago, very much the same. Although I was very different from Sol, we became friends. There were a few "macho" guys in our outfit. In my experience I found them wherever I went. I noticed immediately the one or two who decided to pick on me. For whatever reason, Sol and Sidney may have seemed too easy. How I didn't seem too easy to them I can't understand, but in their plan to pick on one of the Jews, it turned out to be me. The challenge came from one of the guys. They probably flipped a coin. There were acres of wooded areas where no one could see what was going on unless you were there on the spot. Only a few guys gathered around. I don't think they were Jew haters. I just think they wanted to see a fight so they stood by silently. My opponent was at least a head taller than I and made it known that he hated Jews and he was going to show the other guys how to take care of Jews. To describe the fight doesn't matter. Its purpose, Jew hater. Triumphant, I came out of it with a red swollen cheek. Stokes was kneeling on the ground. I didn't stop to see how badly he was hurt. I started back to the barracks with some of the guys walking with me. A couple of guys patted me on the back. Were they Protestant who hated Catholics or Catholics who hated Protestants or are they non-believers like me, or is "might" their god? Whatever they are, I think they're stupid and can easily be swayed to think and believe anyone with a one point higher IQ than they have. I heard later that Stokes had to go to the infirmary.

We're not kids anymore, one could say. Back then as kids I had to fight because I am a Jew. What did we know? We're grown now and like then, my only choice was to defend myself the only way my opponents choose to settle problems they themselves create. I'm glad Mom and Pop can't see me now.

How would they be able to explain this to me. Can you?

There was no shouting to attract attention. After all, getting caught meant six months in the guard house. At morning roll call Captain Couty walked past me silent for a second as he looked at me. "What happened?" he asked. "I fell, sir," I said a little painfully. I knew he didn't believe me. When Stokes didn't answer to the call of his name the Captain knew too of my disadvantage. It was his purpose to keep harmony in our own company so he warned everyone that any in-company fighting will bring a two-year prison term, not the usual six month sentence, and if anyone wanted to fight, to pick on someone in another company and on a contest basis.

When we returned to our barracks I waited for everyone to get settled. My bunk was the first as you entered the door and being in an upper I could oversee the entire hut of 32 men. I rapped on my helmet that hung on the bunk post. Some looked my way, but I needed everyone's attention so I picked up my tommy gun and pulled back on the bolt. The sound of cocking a weapon, especially a tommy gun, has a frightening sound and, at this point, the silence became deafening. I began my announcement. "I don't intend to fight every jerk who gets the whim. With my taped clips I can get off 100 rounds in seconds. Your religion may have taught you to beat up or kill Jews because that's what seems to be the sport so just forget what the Captain said this morning about prison. My ruling will take place before his and I'd just as soon pull this trigger now as later and kill as many of you fuckin' assholes as there are rounds in my clips. You won't know the time I'll pick like maybe now. You guys decide if it's worth it." For an hour or more I sat on my bed, my gun pointing down the room with my finger on the trigger. In the silence that followed I thought of the coincidence that Captain Couty should have given me this weapon when I joined the MPs. For the hour or more, the men, out of fear, never moved from their beds. Everyone relaxed when I moved the bolt forward and engaged the safety.

I don't know how many times I asked myself, "Why?" Even in the school yard so many years ago. Did I miss an explanation along the way. Certainly if there was one after 2000 years Pop

138

would have been able to tell me how to accept this persecution. I know it isn't fair to place all Christians in the category of bigots or Jew killers, but why don't those who aren't stop the others before they themselves are included. If they believe in "might makes right," they could be dead right. What comes to mind is the plight of the blacks who, under the sign of the same cross, were put into slavery and made to accept the Christian God. Of course, there are some who didn't, but I would think if I had been in their plight, in chains and under the whip and sometimes the noose of their Christian master, I could not and would not accept his God for mine. If, before this carnage, the black people had a belief, why didn't they stay with it? Surely they can see all other beliefs vying for first place using murder to insure their gains.

I would like to put this God thing to rest, although I don't believe it ever will since God and religion are so misused. I have heard it so many times. When one emerges unhurt from an accident like a plane crash and says, "God saved me." If God was present at the crash as people say and believe, would it have been too much for God to save the other believers? How about the children killed in this same crash? Why or how can you believe God chose this person above all the others – nonsense. I have been to Jewish services and non-Jewish services and I would hear the Rabbi or Pastor or Priest say "We (man) were made in the image of God." It's hard to accept this since no one ever knew what God looked like and there we go calling God a person instead of a faith. Science has shown our likeness to be that of the ape or gorilla. We could have come from them. If so, am I then to believe God looked like a gorilla? Let's be honest with ourselves. God is only a feeling and if that feeling helps you get through the day don't let it go. Just don't hurt anyone who believes in a stone or even a cloud and respect the person who doesn't believe at all. He just could be a better person than the God believer.

It's unfortunate that my beating Stokes obsessed the guys with the feeling that might is right. I guess they'll never learn.

There are too many weak people who are easily overpowered by crafty soothsayers who find it easy to manipulate people into believing whatever the hawker wants. They should put hallelujah aside for a minute to see where they're being led.

The fight I had with Stokes had a rippling effect on the company. It surely must have gotten to the captain and yet not a word from the old man. Maybe he felt this fight was the final answer.

On all hikes and forced marches our company went on, because of my natural short step, I found it difficult to keep up with the longer legged guys. Also, unaware to me, I had a flat-footed gait. I don't know who started it but someone said I walk like a duck. Almost at once I was nicknamed, "The Duck." It was a fad of sorts among regular army to nickname favorites in one's outfit. Again, it could have been the fight that earned me the nickname. I was never to hear my given name again except at roll call, and at mail call the mail caller would say, "One for the duck." At one time, someone referring to me while talking to the captain said I was nickname "the Duck." It was one time I saw the captain smile. He rarely did. On our next hike and all others that followed, the captain had me take up the rear. Then I did it my way. Nicknames were usually reserved for the army regulars like Albert, known to all as the 'Pig." He lived in the bunk below me. Pig was short and stocky. His head seemed round and oversized and large for his body, but mainly he had a large flat nose with prominent nostrils. No wonder he got stuck with a name like Pig. There was "Moose" another regular who was the biggest man in the company with a deep voice. A sight to behold was "Horse Cock." In the shower you found yourself staring and wondering if it was real. Of course, when someone would call out for him they'd just say "Horse." There were others, five or six. You had to be special. Again, I never knew how or who started it, but Mitzie got the name of "Daisy Mae." At mail call Herb would call out, "Letter from Daisy Mae for the Duck."

Chapter 55

Sol and I became good friends and I became a little more friendly too with some of the others. One particularly was Angelo, "Angie." Angelo was a very quiet guy, almost a loner. He was a short stocky fellow, soft spoken, and his contribution to conversation was mostly about his family and the things he did before the army caught him. His one prominent feature were the two dimples, large and deep, that appeared on his rounded cheeks when he smiled. We'd talk many times and he'd drive me crazy talking about the Italian food dishes his mother would make. But behind all the conversation I could feel Angelo was bothered about war. I guess he was obsessed with the thought of getting killed. I was too and so were the others. Some of the guys are very sensitive and unknowingly show it. He would ask what I thought knowing my thoughts weren't any different than his or anybodys. We would end all conversation with, "it's gonna be all right." Even when we passed one another we would say in unison, "It's gonna be all right."

In the days and times I would be off duty, two or three of the guys and I would go to nearby towns. There was, of course, New Castle where we embarked. North of our camp was Downpatrick and not too far from there was the town of Neury. All these towns were small with nothing to do in them, but just getting away from camp was some diversion. Talking to the townspeople it sometimes was almost painful trying to understand them through their thick accent. There was a fish and chips shop. Imagine holding your fish and chips in a newspaper that served as a plate. The war and shortages were to blame.

We called them "honey dippers." The war shortages prompted the local farmers to gather the human waste from 18,000 men to spread to nourish the growth of their potato fields.

It was only at times when we bought the fish and chips in the towns of Downpatrick or Neury that the thought crossed my mind and I would lose my desire to eat.

We joked about it many different ways and some of the guys would comment on how much better the fries were now than before we came to Ireland and billeted at New Castle.

Once with a weekend pass Sol and I went to Belfast. In one of their best hotel dining rooms the best choice on the menu was a baked bean sandwich. I should mention that from time to time I was lucky at poker. I kept some of the money and sent the rest of my winnings home. That way it would help Mom and I could never lose it back again.

If you had to like being in the army I guess I was in a part of it that was as good as any. We knew we lucked out with our Mess Sergeant. Everything he prepared was good. That in itself made being here tolerable. Word got out about his skill and some officers managed to steal him away.

An introduction to our new Mess Sergeant wasn't necessary. At breakfast one morning his creamed chipped beef on a slice of bread earned its proper name, S.O.S. Around the world S.O.S. is a signal indicating distress, properly name for Joe Moss "Shit on a Shingle." Chocolate pudding was rare, but when we got it, it was always burnt as was almost everything he prepared. We nicknamed him, but not out of love. "Slumburner" Joe Moss. Even though a lot of good food was left untouched, no attempt to remove him was ever made. A treat by comparison for us was on maneuvers when our food was K or C rations.

In addition to inedible food, I was being introduced to foods that can't even be identified. Maybe it's the way Sergeant Moss prepares it. Everything can't possibly be, as the group calls it, "shit." We're all surprised one morning to see what looks like butter. A treat we hadn't seen since becoming soldiers. We learned quickly that it was hard to spread, had no taste and even with a match held to it, it wouldn't melt. We called it axle grease. We were being introduced to margarine.

Chapter 56

Rations like cigarettes, soap, toothpaste and other items were free and available every two weeks at the PX (post exchange). The man behind the counter was disliked by many for his arrogant ways of dispensing the items. He would sometimes toss them at the guys who would try catching as he tossed. For officers, of course, he'd place them on the counter. He was told many times not to throw the items. If he knew you, he'd place them. If he didn't he would throw or toss. Most didn't like it, but didn't do anything to stop him.

The line was long and slow. Some of the things thrown were missed and had to be picked off the floor. At my turn the first couple of items came with the remark, "Catch, Jew boy." The soap in his hand was thrown with the intention to hurt, but the big hurt for me was, "Catch, Jew boy" with each item. I leaned over the counter, grabbed his shirt while pulling him to me and let fly a fist to his face. As he fell behind the counter the men cheered. Unseen by me because of the long and curved line, was a chicken colonel who saw me swing at the counter man. He had me at attention and ordered me to barracks arrest. Minutes later Captain Couty entered the hut. I told him how it happened and that I would like to have a chance to get this incident to the general. The captain knew this chicken colonel and said I'd never get to see the general because I would have to go through the colonel to get to the general and this colonel was no better than the guy behind the counter. The captain said he would take care of it. I was taken off barracks arrest the next morning and as the weeks went by I heard nothing more about the incident. I learned later that no charges were filed and also there was no throwing of rations any more.

Chapter 57

Rumors of us being called to combat are stronger and more frequent. We knew it would be any day soon when a part of the 5th Division gathered on the parade ground to listen to a speech by General Patton. The only memorable part of the general's wisdom was his emphasis on killing the German Nazis and when they turn and run he said, "Shoot them in the ass." The few days that followed had us preparing unlike any other alert. Electric hair trimmers were handed out for all heads to be trimmed to the skin. If you thought these guys were ugly with hair, you should see them now. Anything that could be used for identification except dog tags were to be burnt. Letters from home, pictures, gifts. Angelo came by my bunk. "Could this be a dry run?" I had to tell him I didn't think so since Patton took the time to visit with us. It was red alert very early the next morning. Lt. Bonifedi was officer in charge of our group. We were some 30 men and six jeeps, five men crammed in a jeep with all our gear. We formed a line awaiting the order to drive onto the ramp leading into the liberty ship at the dock in Belfast. Bonifedi, a little obsessed with his rank, wanted to show leadership by shouting out, "I want to see all vehicles move in unison when I say go." We used to humor the lieutenant on occasion, knowing that was what he liked. Obviously, he never had six jeeps in a row start off as though they were one. All drivers listened attentively as he bellowed, "go." The crash, bumper on bumper, could be heard all over the dock. Lt. Bonefedi who was in the lead jeep and wanting to avoid embarrassment, moved into the ship and we followed.

Chapter 58

It's D plus 30 and we're headed for the beaches of Normandy. The crossing is very rough. Most of the men are seasick. Those men near the side rail are heaving their guts out as the ship rolls and dips. We're so crowded the men who can't get to the rail are vomiting where they sit. Our ship stopped about a half mile from the beach and landing craft are already alongside. Two German aircraft coming our way with tracer bullets streaming at us as we crouch for cover. Luckily, ground fire made them veer off and we began groping our way down the gang rope ladder with one eye on the ropes to see where to place a foot and another aimed at the bouncing landing craft below and an eye on the returning German planes. We were pretty well occupied, but not enough to look to my side to see Angelo next to me. As we descended we both said as one, "Nothing to worry about." Maybe it was underwater shifting sand or the landing craft master just missing his landing point, but we emerged from the LST in water up to our chests. It was getting dark. The heavy black clouds that hung over us all day contributed to the darkness earlier than usual. I can see where timing and speed is so important. Oh, I should mention, I am now a PFC. I got the promotion when I went to school some weeks before our invasion to learn the phonetic alphabet for a special job. I emerged from the surf dripping. I was almost as wet sweating from fright before I got into the LST. One was as bad as the other. A jeep was at hand for me on the beach. The transmittal/receiver took up the entire back seat. Turning the dials to lock in on a frequency I suddenly heard music that came from the United States - an indication of the power of the unit. Pig was already in the jeep. On this mission we were partners. With maps showing our locations we were ready to go into no man's land when out of the darkness driving up to our jeep, Captain Couty called to us to hold off. In other similar tries, German radar and artillery were able to pick off vehicles like ours – our mission was scrubbed.

Chapter 59

The Germans are only three miles away. Unlike "D" Day, they had time to reinforce their positions with tanks, guns and men. It wasn't going to be easy. If their reinforcements are great enough, they could easily drive us back into the sea. In our foxholes the first night, nobody could sleep. We would peek above our shallow dugout momentarily, always expecting the enemy to be there. Every now and then a rifle shot rang out – someone thought he was able to make out a moving object in the blinding darkness. With the morning light, the object turned out to be a cow. Some gunfire was at nothing – just nervous soldiers. We moved out that morning, clearing a wooded area and arriving at an open field. Some advance guards were out ahead of us to make sure everything ahead was clear. I sat down on a short tree stump waiting with the rest of our group to move out, when suddenly the crack of a rifle shot pierced the stillness – the sniper's bullet hitting the stump between my legs. To our left, for the length of a city block, was a row of houses. I yelled, "Sniper," at the same time hitting the ground. I was able to catch from the corner of my eye, a figure in a white shirt disappearing into one of the houses. The words "white shirt" relayed quickly and when we caught up with the advance guards, one of them said he just killed someone in a white shirt. Well in advance, civilians who chose to stay in their homes were warned to stay indoors. The wise guy who tried to be a hero will never get a medal.

Instead of moving on, the order came to dig in. I guess we're going to stay a while. Joe Bass, with his group from Signal Company, came by – they were on a wire laying detail. "Polsky is dead – got hit on the beach by artillery." I felt drained. What a waste. We were on the outskirts of Cherbourg and it was off limits to all Army personnel. Pappy had been drinking some wine he picked up on the way. "I'm going into town," he said. With snipers hidden among the townspeople, the off limits order was mainly for our benefit. Being our Top Sergeant, no one would question him or try to stop him. He was a loner, never letting anyone get close to him. Word came some hours later that Pappy had gotten into a fight with a civilian and killed him. He was arrested and we never heard of him again.

Ahead of us was the city of St. Lo. It was heavily fortified and word got to us that the Germans were to hold the city at all costs. Fear of stiff resistance from the Germans can only mean heavy casualties for us but our high command had a mission planned that would calm and hopefully lessen the fear which again gripped us all. Our orders were to dig in about five miles from the city and to prepare to see a spectacle for the first and maybe the last time ever. To lay in our foxholes face up, and at no time attempt to rise above ground level. The spectacle was going to be the bombing of St. Lo by 10,000 planes. We all thought of that number as being over-exaggerated, but as the prearranged time approached, we could see in the distant sky what looked like a swarm of locusts. As that swarm dropped their bombs and moved on, another swarm approaching from another point could be seen. A third and fourth and fifth swarm followed, and then more. A sight, unbelievable as it seemed, but there it was. The thundering sound and the trembling of the ground we lay in, convinced us that indeed, even as far as five miles, this spectacle was taking place. As these different groups of airplanes departed their target, some groups flew right over us. We could see, but were not able to count their numbers. We walked into a city of rubble hardly a building was left standing and not a live German in sight. The news of this day too, was Captain Couty's promotion to Major.

Chapter 60

Looming before us, and never hearing of them before, were the 'Hedge Rows,' a natural obstacle for us and an excellent defensive barrier for the enemy. For a week or so, we couldn't move. The 8th Air Force was called in to bomb the Germans out. Instead of hitting the enemy, they hit us. Properly named "friendly fire." Were we too close or was their aim too poor? We'll never know. The hedge rows had us pinned down. Living in a foxhole for a week or more, doing natural things one has to do in an abnormal way is one dirty experience. Word filtered down one day that a sergeant from some outfit devised a method of fastening huge sharp blades on the front of tanks and cutting their way through the hedge rows. It worked. The tremendous growth was cut to shreds along with Germans if they couldn't get out of the way fast enough.

From St. Lo to the city of Chartres we encountered German "dirty tricks" fighting. Word spread through the division – "no prisoners." It was a bad week for Germans. Our generals, quite angry, finally convinced our front line men that information was drying up and how important it was to take prisoners. We recalled General Patton telling us to shoot the Germans in the ass when they started to run. When prisoner taking resumed we learned from them that the Germans had given the Red Diamond Division (our 5th Division insignia) the name "Red Devils," and it drove fear into those who faced us. Still, our losses were heavy by the time we took the City of Chartres.

Chartres was a warehouse city for the many things stolen from many countries by the Germans. Looting was very heavy, especially among the officers of all units of the Third Army in this area. I was among ten to 20 MPs ordered to go into the city to try to stop the looting. It was an impossible task. We didn't even try. I stopped one soldier and asked him what he was going to do with the grandfather clock he was carrying on his back. "Just going to show the guys what they missed by not coming with me."

Walking back to my headquarters I encountered two guys

from Company L, the outfit I transferred from. "Max Aisen is dead. Their kitchen was hit on some road outside of Cherbourg," they said. Once again I felt that same sickening feeling. Better luck is what we need. Prayers just don't work.

Our new kitchen after a week or more had caught up to us and just outside the headquarters (in an old nearby devastated house) they were setting up to give us our first hot food since landing on the beach. I sat in a ditch along the side of the road eating and thinking of Max and Polsky. I guess the one thought uppermost in our minds is how to get home alive and in one piece. I have seen battlefield scenes in the movies, but there's no comparison when I find myself living it and standing in the middle of this devastation and death. The nauseating smell that adds to all this realism is an experience I will never forget.

It looks like God took the afternoon off for the guys who thought God was on his side. I can hear the whish of bullets passing my ears, waiting for the one that hits.

Chapter 61

From here on, for some of us combat MPs, war was going to be different. Groups of five men will be sent into areas along a wide front to precede a fighting force to direct them to prevent straggler groups from entering pockets of impossible situations that have turned around in favor of the Germans. We found ourselves many times in enemy territory and expendable. One of these situations was in the deserted town of Novient in Alsace Lorraine in a valley along a narrow point of the Moselle River. On the opposite side of the river, just 500 yards in front of us, was high ground held by the Germans. From their vantage point they could see every move we made. Even as we rode into town, their artillery shells started exploding around us. All the guys in our jeep scampered to whatever cover could be found. I jumped into a gas station grease pit only a few feet from where our jeep stopped. I hoped there wasn't any gasoline in the pumps. From out of nowhere, Major Couty appeared on a motorcycle. From the high ground on our side, miles away, he could see the exploding shells being lobbed in on us. The Major knew we had no medics attached to our group. If there were casualties he wanted to help. For cover he rode into the gas station where I had taken cover. In the excitement of the bombarding I forgot myself and said, "What the hell are you doing here – this place is hot." The major yelled out, "Is everybody all right?" "We don't know," I shouted back. At this point, the major understood that movement drew the German fire. I guess the major thought he'd use himself as a target so with tremendous speed on his bike he rode out, drawing more shells at him and away from us. Our group leader, Sergeant Cunningham, called to us to stay hidden where we were until dark. The Germans might think their artillery got us all. A frightening situation for us to think about as the major realized, is the fact that we had no medics in the event any of us was wounded. Lucky for us there was no moon this night. Out of fear that noise would give us away we pushed the jeep down an alley, putting it behind a house out of sight, and decided to take that house for shelter. We were put here to direct

153

other units away from this point. What about us? Coming in with no way to get out, I guess we were trapped. If we were forced to be there beyond tomorrow we would be out of rations. There wasn't time to replenish rations for this mission and if the Germans decided to cross the river to check on us we wouldn't need any.

In one of our huddles to discuss our position and figure out what to do, we came up with zero. We were cut off from communications and from our latest information we were right in the middle of what could be a pre-planned counterattack initiating from the German side.

In the cellar of the house where we were was a pile of rotted potatoes crawling with rats. I guess we won't have any of them for dinner tonight. It was Day Two when Sergeant Cunningham decided to crawl out in the yard to get an idea of our position. Laying low behind the house he was fairly safe, but the sergeant was unable to come up with any escape plan. On his way back as he crawled slowly, he chanced upon the chicken that had been roaming in the yard. With lightning speed he reached out and caught the chicken's leg. The cackling was so loud we hoped the Germans across the river didn't hear it. Cunningham brought the chicken in and, holding it said, "Would you like this for lunch or dinner?" We just weren't prepared for a joke. Nobody laughed. Besides, dinner many times came in the morning or any time. The big and new problem came when someone had to volunteer to kill the chicken. We looked at one another for a moment or two with no one volunteering. It might have been easier to decide if it were a German chicken, but Alsace Lorraine, it had to be French. On the floor, where Cunningham sat when he crawled in, reached and opened the door and let the chicken go.

In an after thought, building a fire to cook the chicken would alert Germans that we were still alive. Letting the chicken go may have saved the chicken's life and ours. Maybe someday this incident will reach the "Reader's Digest" as one of my most unforgettable experiences in the war. We were extremely quiet and through the day and night we placed a guard outside. We too listened for noise that could tell us something. On the night of day three Sol, who was on guard at the road that went past the house, came in saying he heard what sounded like a shuffling of feet. A pig had been roaming the area, but we decided not to take chances. We huddled again and decided the Germans heard the chicken yesterday and were sending in a squad to check if we were still alive. We took up positions at windows and doors. We were vulnerable. It would only take a hand grenade to finish us off so being very quiet might save our lives. The night was pitch dark. Sol was right. We heard the shuffling of feet and some body movement as the German patrol passed our house. We stayed in our positions for at least 20 minutes when we heard repeated gun and automatic gun fire. There was no way to know what was happening down the road. We stayed awake through the whole night, still being very quiet, should the German patrol return. This is day four or five and I'm beginning to think something is wrong with me. I stopped being hungry. It's late afternoon and Sergeant Cunningham called for another huddle.

We decided to make a run for it, banking on the premise that a moving target is difficult to hit so we went in our jeep from behind the house out onto the road and back up the hill from where we came. I had pulled out the speedometer needle stop some time ago. We were exceeding the 60 miles per hour that was printed on the gauge as the shells from the German side burst just behind us. Lucky for us we were a little bit out of their range.

About a quarter of a mile up the road on our race out we saw the German patrol from the other night sprawled out all over the road, dead. The gun fire that we heard the other night we learned at last came from the 5th Division mortar outfit that moved into an area not far from us and ambushed the German patrol.

Major Couty was aroused again by the artillery fire and through binoculars watched us outrun the shells. He was there to see that we were all right. The best menu offered us was our choice of C rations. I don't know what part of the day it was, but after our banquet our group slept till the following morning.

Chapter 62

Our jeep caught some damage from the shelling in Novient and was declared out of use. The last run we made in it was its last. We stood in dismay at the new vehicle presented to us for our transportation – a captured German half-track. This had to be the dumbest idea yet. With the rivalry that I think goes on among our own officers, I wonder if this isn't the colonel's chance to shove it to Major Couty. It had to come from someone close to the top command, someone stupid. In combat a soldier learns to distinguish the enemy, especially at night, by sound. I don't know any American soldier in this war who wouldn't shoot first if he thought it was the enemy, and ask questions later.

We were off on our new mission the next morning in our very noisy German half track. We drove on roads shown on our maps and, at times having to take detours because of impassable roads. In the still of the night we knew our half track could be heard for miles in all directions. It was midnight. A rifle shot out of the darkness hit our vehicle and we stopped and turned off the motor. It was then we heard someone shout, "Halt." I thought it only happened in the movies, but in the darkness, by voice only, we were asked the password, then the names of baseball players and their respective teams. I knew one and Sergeant Newman knew another. We were ordered out of the vehicle and told to walk toward the tiniest, almost pin-point, light. It took about 50 steps when we were stopped and we were standing in front of three 75 millimeter cannons poised to fire on us. The major in charge of the artillery outfit told us our objective was over run and didn't exist any more. Communications verified this and we stayed put, pending new orders.

Chapter 63

We got our new orders by morning. The artillery captain assisted us, using a map overlay to show us the best way to get to Rhiems if the Germans hadn't retaken the area. Fifth Division infantry troops were to be there about the time we were due to arrive, but again, like many times before, we were all alone. We drove up and stopped in the square of the Rhiems Cathedral.

Our mission was to keep our own invading troops from looting the Piper Heidsieck Champagne warehouse. A little way down the road in the opposite direction was a bridge that crossed another part of the Moselle River and just on the other side of the bridge were the Germans. We were only five MPs on this side and a German army just across the bridge. I guess we have to be thankful for a German snafu if they are thinking a very large force was now facing them. It was nightfall that gripped us with fear. We waited until dusk to set our side of the bridge with hand grenade booby traps. When all seemed in order we sat down on the steps of the Rhiems Cathedral. Chapman took first guard, well hidden, a half block down the road facing the bridge.

Chapman was a first line soldier of Company K. It was the slaughter in one of the battles back in Cherbourg that so frightened him that he deserted. He wound up in one of our prison barbed wire enclosures awaiting the consequences of a court martial. It was back when the Major was Captain and he feared he might be too low in rank to try to help this shivering and frightened soldier. But he tried and was successful in getting Chapman released in his custody and responsibility. In all these past months of hell we went through Chapman became hardened in a human sort of way and, although still frightened, proved to be a good and dependable soldier. Major Couty proved to us all that he was a good judge of character and a man with a caring heart.

There were homes along the rim of the square and, as the guys settled down, a man and two members of his family appeared carrying a large tray of vegetables. His daughter spoke English, thanking us for rescuing them from the Boshe. We thanked them for the vegetables and told them to stay indoors, not to come out again until we told them they could. We all took our turn to stand guard through the night. There was no enemy action this night.

With daylight we positioned ourselves near the warehouses and signs of our main force started to appear. I took my turn to patrol one side of the warehouse while Chapman took the opposite side. It was a great relief knowing a bigger force was now here in the event there should be a German counterattack. Halfway down the street I noticed an officer coming in my direction. I first noticed his captain's bars and as he came closer I knew at once who he was. My old Company Commander of Company L, Captain Carl. He didn't recognize me and I decided to leave it that way. I wondered if he still hated Jews. "Sir," I said, "this area is off limits to all personnel. You'll have to leave." As I expected, the Captain hadn't changed and with an authoritative sound in his voice said, "I came to get some wine for my men and I'm giving you an order to back off." I did take a few steps backward, took my tommy gun that was slung over my shoulder and lowered it, at the same time pulling back on the bolt. I thought to myself, "What better way to rid the world of another Jew hater and whatever other people this man hated." The Captain appeared stunned and stood still for some seconds, then turned to leave. As he turned he said, "My report will read you disobeyed a direct order under combat conditions." He had only taken a few steps when I called out, "You forgot to ask me my name, sir. It's Private First Class Martin Tucker. Remember?" With more of the main force rapidly coming up other outfits were deployed to take our place and we were relieved of our mission.

Chapter 64

With the map coordinates given us we found the designated area. It didn't look like another mission. It looked like a farm with one house on the entire grounds. We may have been given a few days rest since there were no orders at the time we arrived and we were some 20 miles behind the front lines. Some hundred or so yards off to the side of the farm house was a most ominous sight. Lined up were eight 155 millimeter long toms, each about 20 yards apart. Some men belonging to the artillery outfit were sitting on the porch when we drove up. A lieutenant hailed us saying he was expecting us and told us we could have the second floor of the house. We settled down. It was like being on vacation in the country. We weren't advised of what was going to happen. Maybe the artillery people didn't know either until the order came. Without any announcement, gun number 1 opened fire. One minute later gun number 2 fired and so on down the line and then the volley repeated. With each firing the house shook and rattled like it would if we were having an earthquake. The firing continued throughout the night. We were given ear plugs, but the house shaking added to the sleepless night. The guns were still firing into late morning and as we stood outside watching the big guns blazing away, the house collapsed in front of our eyes. By this time in the war we traveled very light. There were no belongings to search for in the rubble and, lucky for us, we weren't in the house when it caved in. The guns stopped sometime in the afternoon. That night we slept outside. Some vacation!

Chapter 65

Orders came for us to join headquarters and a part of the division's main force. We were advancing rapidly at this time unopposed and coming out of a wooded area our convoy abruptly stopped. In front of us and atop a high sloping hill was a German pill box. From a point where I stood I could see the white flash of gun fire coming from the narrow slit opening. We all took cover behind trees and vehicles. Major Couty came by angrily shouting, I don't have time for volunteers," pointing a finger to three men. "You, you and you," and turning to me said, "Give me your gun." A colonel crouched behind his command car ordered the MPs to take the pill box. The major had every right to be angry. Up ahead were two weapons carriers and one anti-tank vehicle that could more easily have managed the encounter than four men with only hand weapons. (It's another sign of inside brass hatred and rivalry.) For the Germans in the pill box it was like shooting fish in a barrel. From where we stood we could see our men clearly since they had no cover while hugging the ground shooting at the pill box slit. Some signal company guys who were laying wire just behind the pill box heard the German machine guns firing and turning in that direction were able to see the gun fire raking the field below. From behind they crawled up to the sides of the pill box slit and silenced the gunners with a couple of hand grenades. On his return the major said, "Barnes and Thomas were killed." He handed me my gun saying, "It had to be cleaned." I always felt that the major save my life by taking my gun and not me.

Chapter 66

Many times we found ourselves in enemy territory. If a river separated us we could most times see the Germans on the opposite side which meant they were able to see us, always a scary situation.

In most cases when we were given a mission to perform we were told its purpose. If conditions have changed by the time we reach our point, we're on our own. To try to figure out the thinking behind some missions would sometimes have us wondering if the brass knows what it's doing. For what it's worth, if anything went wrong the loss would only be our lives.

One of those missions that we concluded had no purpose showed up on the front page of nearly every newspaper in the United States the day after we reached our target. It was "First U.S. Troops Enter the City of Frankfort." One of the guys got a letter from home telling us all about it some weeks later.

Those U.S. troops were five Fifth Division MPs. The city appeared to be very big as we drove cautiously on empty streets. Not a person in sight --- and again the fear of snipers. The dot on our map brought us to a bridge and on the opposite side of the bridge were the Germans. We hid our jeep and made ourselves obscure too, although I'm sure the Germans knew we were there. If they decide to cross the bridge we'd have no choice but to surrender. Surely we couldn't survive any attack.

We were sent here expecting we would arrive in conjunction with the main force. However, we huddled to decide what to do in case of this or that and for three or four hours we were all alone.

Like many times before, the Germans may have been overly cautious, thinking we were the advance of a large force and trying to cross a bridge could be a foolish decision. It would be dark in another hour. The Germans could be waiting for the night to make their move. After all, the City of Frankfort is a big prize. Hand grenades are our biggest weapons. Not much good if they send tanks. As Sergeant Cunningham was starting to say something about us being alone, the rumble from our side turned

165

into the pouring in of our Fifth Division troops from all sides. Once again luck was on our side and again the feeling of relief.

There were no news people to record this event, maybe because it was too dangerous. Had they been here with us they would have learned the names of those five MPs Sergeant Cunningham, Sol, Anderson, Pig and me.

Chapter 67

The Fifth Division had been a spearhead since Normandy and we were preparing ourselves to walk into Paris. Some of the guys are even excited about it and the chance to write home about something special. Rumor was that we might stay a few days. It wasn't to be. We got the order to stop on the outskirts of the city. A moment of pride was here and the important people that make decisions said the Free French had earned the right to walk into and retake their own city.

We skirted Paris and continued with the war. The Germans left the city intact and so life continued there almost uninterrupted. One night as we lay in our fox holes news filtered through our area that four-day passes to Paris would be given out. (Names in alphabetical order.) My last name with the letter "T" meant I'd never get the chance to go. Pig, whose real name I never knew, called out to me from his fox hole that I could go in his place since he didn't care to see Paris. It didn't matter, but Pig's last name I learned from the other guys was Bower.

In the dark of the following night I crawled out of my fox hole with six or eight other guys, got in a truck and, after being given some money (in French francs) we were off to Paris. The gaiety of the newly freed city and its people added to the declared holiday that was still going on when I arrived. I really wasn't that much in the mood. I was very tired and my first thought was a long overdue shower and sleep. A young girl showed me to my room in a side street hotel. She said her name was Fanny and she offered other services which I declined. The surprised look on her face matched the remark she made in French. As she was instructed, she told me in English where I could go for food, to the Red Cross dining room in a larger hotel down the street. Meals there for servicemen were free. Fanny walked me down the hall to show me the community bathroom. She was halfway down the hall and said, "If you want me call the desk downstairs." Everything in the hotel looked old, but clean. This was probably a second or third class hotel. The bathroom, out of necessity, was my first priority. The toilet had an overhead water container near the ceiling. A long chain hung from it for flushing. I had seen this contraption before, but next to the toilet was one I had never seen before. It had no seat or chain and was smaller than a normal looking toilet. There was a peddle on the floor next to the fixture that I was guessing was a way to flush this thing. I had never seen anything like it. Looking into the bowl to watch it flush, I pressed down on the peddle with my foot. The shot of water hit my face as I quickly leaned back to avoid the surprise. This thing worked in reverse. I had to see it one more time. Leaning back I pressed the peddle. The fountain almost hit the ceiling. As I was preparing to leave the hotel I noticed Fanny at the desk and she explained the contraption in the bathroom. She probably thinks I'm a hick from Hicksville.

We were given $25 in francs. I didn't know one bill from another. I would have to depend on a Frenchman's honesty to take the right amount from my hand for whatever I bought. I was only interested in sightseeing. Trolley and bus fare were my biggest expenditures. On day two or three I got lost. I drew a picture of the Eiffel Tower for some French natives I was asking for help. I remembered my hotel being several blocks from the Eiffel Tower so I used it as a reference point. The French people who tried to help me understood my drawing, but I couldn't understand them as they tried to direct me. Seeing two men on a street corner I decided to speak to them in Yiddish and, to my surprise, they understood me and I at last was able to find my way back to my hotel.

I was digging a new fox hole and thinking of the past four days I had just spent. Pig wanted to know if he missed anything by not going. I told him, "No." It would take more than $25 to have a really good time in Paris.

It appears my biggest excitement was the bidet.

The war had not taken a holiday, but at this point the Germans were running a little faster. We had just taken this small town outside of Paris and were well on our way to take the next when Sergeant Newman, Chapman, Moose and I were ordered to rush back to the last town to quell a disturbance that had erupted. The name of the town, like many others, was unidentifiable since early bombing or shelling may have blown their signs away.

We pulled up in the midst of the melee to see the townspeople stoning four girls corralled in a horse-drawn cart. The girls' hands were tied to the top rung of the cart, their clothes partially torn from their bodies and, with heads shaven, we knew the angry natives were venting their wrath on the girls who in the past had fraternized with the Germans. It took several shots into the air to persuade the locals to back off and calm down.

We untied the girls and stayed with them until the proper authorities could take charge and hopefully keep the girls out of danger.

Riding back to join our company I wondered what drove these girls to behave as they did. Was it hunger? Were they threatened? They didn't look like politicos who sympathized with the Boshe. I guess there's no way of knowing why about anything but, for sure, everything has a price to pay.

Chapter 68

Winter was setting in although it seemed to be with us all along. I don't ever remember being warm or dry. Since Normandy it rained much of the time. If the sun shone at all I don't remember.

We were headed for the City of Metz. On the German side of the Moselle River, the city and area for miles was fortified with a series of connecting forts. Fort Driant was successful in keeping us pinned down on our side of the river. There appeared to be only one small area for a logical crossing on this front. Their guns kept us from moving up or back in this area called Arniville. The Germans held high ground and again, to their advantage. From our bivouac we took turns pulling duty at our sloping side of Arniville, constantly enduring the bombardment by the Fort Driant guns. On my turn to pull duty at the river front I found, on the sloping side of the hill, an L-shaped fox hole. It obviously was dug by someone before me. I was safe from bursting shells as long as I stayed inside of the opening. From time to time I'd peer out to see what was happening. One could see the activity on both sides from my theater seat. I suppose we were there, poised to repel a German attack should they decide to cross the river to regain the ground they lost.

It was some time later in the day and during a lull in the shelling. I peered out of my shelter just in time to see General Patton with two of his aides drive up in a jeep. He was no more than 20 or 30 feet from me. There was no mistaking him; his two pearl handled revolvers so prominently hanging from his sides and the three stars very prominent on the front of his helmet. I had seen him before during the hedge row fighting for a glimpsing moment, but I remember him well at a field review in Ireland a week before our invasion. I could hear them talking and I developed the usual chill when I heard him say, "We cross the river tomorrow morning." When I got back to the bivouac I told the guys I saw General Patton. "Oh, yeah," said Anderson, "and I saw Betty Grable in the latrine watching me pee." I didn't expect them to believe me so I said nothing about the general's decision.

Crossing the Moselle River and the capture of Fort Driant was considered successful, even though the casualties on our side were very high. The major, along with some of our company, was part of the initial attack.

A group of MPs stayed behind to maintain the barbed wire prisoner enclosure and I was one of them. The offensive was successful, but our casualties were very high. The prisoner catch was big. On this very cold and dark night we had about 100 prisoners corralled. I was on guard duty, stomping my feet in the 10° to 20° below zero cold. It was about 3 AM. From the start of our entrance in the war, capturing and talking to the prisoners (sometimes interrogating), my Yiddish language by now turned to German. I overheard a voice from the prisoner compound that sounded like someone standing next to me. He addressed himself to the other prisoners as an officer and was giving orders for some of them to throw themselves over the barbed wire so others could run over their bodies and in a riot overtake the guards and catch the others who were asleep. I guess he didn't count on my understanding him and in the second he finished blasting his order, I stuck my gun through the barbed wire into his back saying I would kill him and everyone in the compound if he moved or spoke another word. I let them know in a loud voice that I was a Jew and I'd love to kill them all. I said too, "If I hear a sound from anyone I'll open fire." For an hour or so I stood in that one spot. I kicked my right foot with my left and left on my right trying to keep my feet from freezing. The only sound that came from the enclosure was stomping feet. The only one not stomping or moving was the German officer. Anderson was there to relieve me some three hours later. There was a little advantage for him with daylight soon breaking. I gave Anderson my tommy gun should he need a weapon like mine. Anderson continued with my treatment of silence and the gun in the back of the German officer. Later in the day the prisoners were taken to a rear echelon compound. The German officer was hospitalized for frozen feet and when word reached headquarters I was chosen to be placed on field arrest until the situation could be examined to determine the cause that could mean the possible amputation of the German officer's feet. At the inquiry I stated my position and the option I had at the time. The four officers at the table to listen and perhaps judge, talked amongst themselves and then, turning to me a colonel said, "Dismissed." I was still standing in my "parade rest" position and for the few seconds following my dismissal I was angry – angry to have been singled out for arrest and this inquiry.

I was upset at the thought that these, our leaders, would take time out from the war to discuss the situation in which I found myself. (Didn't they give this any thought at all?) It doesn't take that much experience, even for a "West Pointer", to conclude that 100 men could overrun a single guard, even if the guard were able to kill some of the enemy. I had to chance the need to know if I did what common sense urged me to do. While still nervous as hell, I asked if I may ask a question. The colonel appeared startled at my request and after a brief moment said, "Yes." "What would you have done, sir, had you been in my place?" They looked at each other and again the colonel turned to me and gruffly said, "Dismissed."

I returned to our bivouac wondering whose side these officers were on. No decision was reached at my dismissal so it left a lot for me to think about. One fantastic thought came to me – would they send me back to the states to ponder the decision. Wow!

Chapter 69

When Major Couty entered one of the forts he noticed, off in a corner, a German shepherd dog curled up and shivering. The dog was in shock from the shelling and bombing we launched in the many weeks past. He was careful, not knowing how the dog would react. After five minutes or so the dog responded, showing some affection. Mopping up Germans hidden in many of the rooms in the fort who thought they might be overlooked and then escape was a tremendous job. It was from one of the prisoners that the major learned the dog's name was "Luke." Because I spoke some German the major gave me the job of caring for Luke and nursing him back to health. Some of the guys acquired a house for our short stay here in Metz so Luke and I moved in. With a hairbrush I found in one of the rooms I was able to give Luke a treat he hadn't experienced I guess for a long time. And for dinner we both had ham and eggs C ration. I stayed with Luke through the night. I never owned a pet and here I was being nurse to a dog and I loved it. Luke, still shivering, slept quietly through the night, lying close to me with my arm over his neck. In the morning our breakfast was again ham and eggs C ration. I apologized to Luke for the menu. A fancy bowl that I think was a decorative living room piece became Luke's drinking bowl. The major came by to see how we were getting along. Luke licked the major's hand that seemed like a gesture of thankfulness. "I'll take him for awhile," the major said. "You can take a break." The city was now well in our possession and feeling safe, I decided to take a walk down what looked like Main Street. The street, as far as I could see, was deserted. Even our own soldiers were nowhere in sight. The buildings on one side of the street looked like residences. They were about four stories tall. The trolley tracks in the center of the street indicated the city was very big.

The side of the street I was walking on had stores and businesses. I stopped in front of a store that may have been a beauty supply shop. Behind the big plate glass window were displays of perfume and other such items. It was obvious that

175

the townspeople had left in a hurry. They also could be nearby in hiding. Another GI who had the same idea as I of walking around town suddenly appeared. He came up to me and said, "Would you like some of that perfume?" I said "Yes, but the store is locked up." With the butt of his rifle he sent it into the window. "It's open now." He bent down and picked up a bottle, opened it and, like in the movies, dabbed his ears saying, "Wait till the guys smell me now."

I picked up two small bottles, shaking off the glass particles. To myself I said, "I'll save these for Mitzie." As I walked away I thought to myself, "Why couldn't I do what that other guy did?"

Chapter 70

General Patton said we had earned a rest. The Fifth Division gave up their fox holes to the Ninth Division. Some piled into trucks while we were in a jeep headed for a town called Peienns. The last bath I had was in Paris. I remember having had to put on my dirty, smelly clothes after I bathed. I hope there will be clean clothes at this break. No wonder that GI in Metz dabbed his ears. I should have done the same.

Someone in the general's command planned a great party for us. There was all the champagne we could drink, thanks to Piper Heidsieck and, in the muddy streets of this small town, several houses with girls were supplied for those who wanted them. Tickets were given to the soldiers who, upon entering the room, would give his ticket to the girl. She would be paid for her number of tickets by the army, I guess.

It looked like we were late getting here. As we drove into town we could see that several thousand soldiers had already settled down. Some were already staggering down the muddy streets, a bottle in each hand. The house I stayed in also housed about 20 men. I didn't care about anything; just a shower and some hot food, even Joe Moss's. In the shower area a large tent with a shower apparatus was rigged by the engineers. On the way out delousing powder and the quartermaster set up a table with new underwear, undershirt and shirt. Not exactly the Ritz, but very welcome.

Lieutenant Arent was walking toward me and motioned. In one of the girlie houses some of the men were drunk and shooting their guns into the ceiling. Pretty dumb, we agreed, as they could easily kill some of the girls. "We're to go down there and take their guns and put them aside until they're ready to leave." It doesn't look like the MPs are going to get much rest.

The line was long and Tom and I were partners on this detail. Tom stayed downstairs to pick up the guns while I tried to keep order on the second floor. You could see bullet holes in the floor, but luckily no one got hurt. Two naked girls scampered down the hall holding their crotches and yelling,

"Machine kaput." Two guys, pretty drunk, decided they'd share one girl. I shut the door as they went in. Some camera men from Signal Company took pictures of the girls, some of them in action. They said they were going to make duplicates and pass them out to the guys when they go back to their war. Four o'clock was closing time and the girls were happy. They all said they were very sore. None of them showed up the next day. The MPs that I was on duty with never got to join the fun.

Because of the girl thing our rest area was off limits to the newspeople, understandably. If news like this got home many wives of soldiers might not take too kindly to it. But with so many people knowing about it and some soldiers writing home about the affair, some even sending pictures, how long could this be kept out of home town newspapers? In one of our bull sessions the subject came up. Tom added his point of view saying, "Why should there be any negative fuss? Everybody in the United States Army knows our Supreme Commander has a girl friend so why shouldn't we have our few minutes of a good time? If wives trust their husbands at war those guys should stay away. Look at us. All we got was a chance to watch."

My bed partner was again Luke. Believe me, he was a lot prettier than the girls. When I'm with Luke he doesn't leave my side. When I lie down he does too, right next to me, almost touching. I wish I could find some real food for him. These C rations are bad enough for us. The water we drink with the added pills is the water he drinks, poor dog. The major had me stop by his office to work out an arrangement for Luke for the next few days. He wanted to share the load of taking care of him.

On my way back to my house I passed a quartermaster depot. Stacked outside a house-like building were boxes of supplies meant for rear echelon and occupying forces. One of the boxes was ripped open and, to my surprise, the label on the can read, "Spaghetti in Tomato Sauce." With a can in each pocket and one in each hand I hurried out of sight. I thought of Angelo. It's been months since I saw him. He must have pulled duty as I did in this break since I didn't even see him at chow time. Our temporary headquarters showed me how to reach him.

He was only several streets away. "Nothing to worry about," was the greeting when we met. "Look what I found for you," I said, as I held out two cans of spaghetti. I wasn't sure if saw a tear, but the smile and two cheek dimples were as prominent as ever. It was also our first mail call in these past months. Angelo and I exchanged news we got from home. The spaghetti, even though cold, was a real treat.

We spent the next few remaining days trying to keep order in this little town. Many men stayed drunk the entire time. I stashed a bottle of champagne in my bag and I hope to be able to open it to celebrate with Mitzie. The Ninth Division had encountered strong opposition and lost ground so we went back on the line, crawling back this time into their fox holes.

Chapter 71

Once again we're a team of five. Sergeant Newman is in charge. Sergeant Newman was born in Czechoslovakia and was almost a "by the book" sergeant, not tough, always asking our opinion before making a decision. On our new orders, it's the city of Fontainebleu, to direct a group of the fourth Armored Division scheduled to come through the city. The street slants downwards as we enter and we're poised for snipers. It's that scary feeling again, like being the target. At the intersection as drawn on our map, we came to the right spot. On one corner stood a very impressive white stone building, only two stories high. Near the roof and centered on the front of the building hung a huge gold painted swastika held by eagle's claws. Sergeant Newman suggested we check out the building. Two men took cover behind the jeep parked across the street and against the wall to cover us as we entered the building. In the center of the lobby on a marble floor stood a huge bronze statue. Two white marble staircases on opposite sides of the lobby curved upward to the second floor. A center strip of red carpet covered the steps to the top to meet a red carpeted hall. Among all this splendor my heart was beating like a drum, anticipating a surprise German attack. Huge, gold inlaid doors led to rooms all along the hall. Paul hugged the top step to cover for Sergeant Newman and me as we took opposite sides of the hall to investigate. Newman and I, watching one another, simultaneously opened the doors that were in front of us only enough to toss in a hand grenade. I crouched on the floor, slightly away from the door and waited for the dust to settle and entered the room. What a shame. No one was there The grenades just tore up some beautiful furniture. In the room I entered my eye caught two paintings and, disregarding all we were told about booby traps, I took my knife from its sheath and cut the paintings from their frames. I was lucky. I broke the thin flag pole that supported a swastika flag, using it to roll up the paintings. We checked all the rooms, one furnished more elegantly than the other. Newman and I met on the ground floor using side stairways and at a door that led to the cellar we decided to just throw a couple of grenades down instead of going down to check. The building and the entire street appeared empty of people. We agreed that the town was safe.

The Fourth Armored Division rolled in and we directed them to the roads they had to take. Retracing our route, we rejoined our division.

Chapter 72

I can't get used to saluting Lieutenant Arent. Only a month ago he was a sergeant. He was commissioned in the field and, being new to him too, he told the guys they didn't have to salute. But he earned it so, like it or not, we salute. Lieutenant Arent said the major wanted to see me. I'm always nervous about having to see the old man. Not as nervous as I used to get, a feeling, but for only a second grips me. I guess I've been more trouble to him than anyone in the company. I wondered what it was I did wrong now.

"The front line interrogation team needs someone who can speak German for assistance. Headquarters wants an MP for the job and you fit," said Major Couty, adding, "Sorry about that."

I thought of the 180 men in our company and how unusual it appeared that none were of German extraction, maybe someone who could speak German other than me. Maybe, since we're fighting and killing Germans, they didn't want it known who they were. The backlash, even jokingly, would make it a hell for them.

The A patch on their sleeves identified them. I was to guard newly taken prisoners while waiting their turn for interrogation. Also to assist in questioning the prisoners if necessary. I didn't feel qualified for that part of the job, but who's around to hear my complaint.

I could tell immediately by their accent upon introduction, the two American officers in charge were German. The partly shelled barn served as their headquarters. The enemy lines were only 100 yards away. In the four weeks I spent with them I understood why the U.S. army used such people for extracting information from newly captured German soldiers. They were brutal. Their goon-like methods turned my stomach. I hated Germans as much or more than anyone. I have no trouble firing my weapon at Germans when confronted, but not this. When I was asked to participate in their method of questioning I refused and sent a message to Major Couty to get me out of there.

Upon returning and reporting to the major he said he knew I

183

wouldn't like that detail, but had no choice when he chose me. His actions and tone were a sort of again, "I'm sorry it had to be you."

Chapter 73

Our advance came to a halt just outside of a town called Bitburg. No one could understand why since the Germans were running away faster than we were advancing. We spent that night in the field. Some soldiers commandeered a house to spend the night in another part of the town's outskirts. In the morning a seven year old boy was caught bragging about pointing out a house where the Americans were staying to Germans in a panzer tank. The tank wiped out all the GIs who slept there. This wasn't supposed to happen when we learned that the Germans had agreed to withdraw from the town without a fight. That was the reason for halting our advance. The reason became more clear when we learned that Bitburg was a German officer's town. German officers' families lived there and, in order to save the town from destruction, the Germans offered to surrender the town to us. Anticipating our refusal, the entire town was evacuated days before.

Several thousand men moved into Bitburg homes where we were going to stay for a few days. We were already angry about the unnecessary deaths of our men and now we're supposed to handle Germans officers' homes and possessions with care. I'm glad you didn't bet on it. We lived in real luxury just for two days. Some guys slept in beds with sheets even though they didn't take their clothes off. Some used what looked like expensive dishes to eat their rations from and, when finished, smashed them on the floor. The two to three hours we had before moving out was enough time. Furniture and dozens of other things went flying out of windows on to streets and yards. What wasn't moveable in the houses was destroyed to the best of our ability. As we left some fires were started. Some guys rigged booby traps -- a 100% vote to let our brass know how we felt and not to accept terms like this again. This is an enemy that must get back what they dish out and more. If orders like this Bitburg order are coming from Eisenhower, he's losing our respect. Knowing General Patton as he is known among us, an order like this would never have come from him.

Chapter 74

The new assignment is for the entire Fifth Division. Attack the Saar Lautern area in southern Germany. We were about to face the Siegfried line. You'd think by now we'd be hardened enough to face anything without being scared. We rolled with minimum trouble through many small towns the first two days with no opposition. At 3 AM the morning of the third day it seemed like all hell broke loose. There was great commotion in our own division to get up and assemble at a designated point. Trucks were already there to load our men. We were called to race to Luxembourg and Belgium. It was only hours since the start of "The Battle of the Bulge." Except to stop to refuel we rode for 24 hours. The men relieved themselves over the tailgate of the truck even while we rode and no one left the truck even for the few minutes it took to gas up. We entered the City of Luxembourg and immediately went into battle.

This tremendous German counterattack made for a lot of confusion upon entering the battle zone. It's terribly cold and with the deep snow to contend with, we're having problems we haven't begun to work out. There's no time for white clothing to help us blend into the snow so we're easier targets.

The edge of the Black Forest bordered the row of houses that ran up hill for about two city blocks in addition to which its few inhabitants comprised this whole town.

The house at the bottom of the hill had on its first floor a store that was at one time a flourishing butcher shop. It was bare now which was obvious when I entered to check it out. Olga, the daughter of the store's proprietor, was stringing a cow's intestines, zig-zagging on a table almost the length of the store. I assumed she was wearing work clothes, but I couldn't help seeing how the war took its toll here and throughout this small community. Olga called out, apologizing for her messy appearance that I happened upon, and telling me she was preparing to make wurst. Of course, I knew what it was, but Olga, who spoke some English, continued to explain, "It's like your American hot dogs."

Olga's parents who lived above the store, hearing that someone had entered, came down to introduce themselves. I learned that only five or six people remained in the town. Some of the other guys who were also checking must have found that out by this time. On the opposite side of the road was a large field. The major had already begun to construct the barbed wire enclosure to house potential prisoners. I guess this is the area we will settle in for now. The 30° below zero cold was bad enough for us. It must have been unbearable for the few remaining people in the town.

Blakely was gunning his jeep to make it up the hill in the deep snow, in a hurry to show the guys the deer he said he found. He had it stretched over the hood of the jeep. He said that someone, not he, shot the deer, but got it before the hunter could retrieve it. Olga's father, Herman, cut some fine steaks from the carcass for us that we cooked on his wood burning stove. What a treat! We insisted he keep the remainder of the deer for the few townspeople. The natural refrigeration would allow the meat to keep until it was gone.

I had to check some residence in the town for security reasons and also to take as many of the unoccupied houses for our own men. It was as cold in the houses as it was outside, but it was better than lying in the snow. Mrs. Bonner must have been aware of my climbing the stairs to her third floor apartment. I rapped only once on the door as it opened. I spoke to her in German, introducing myself, while she immediately asked me to come in. She held a metal container that looked like a football with a cap that extended from the center top. "Are your hands cold?" she asked. I said yes and with that she handed me the container. It was hot, but not burning. Almost at once I returned it and she then said, "It's my man." It was a bed warmer much like a hot water bottle. I couldn't guess her age, but she could conceivably have been someone's grandmother. This gentle old lady lived alone in this third floor walkup, a dangerous place to be when the shells come lobbing in. She said this was her home and she was too old to run for safety and added, "Where is it safe?" She had already heard about the deer and expressed her gratitude for the gift and invited me to stay for a cup of hot cocoa.

The German surprise attack was only one of the actions that threw the Americans off guard. The thing that caught us unaware was the fact that the Germans were dressed in American uniforms. They knew who they were while we thought they were our guys. Many of them were hand-picked SS troops who could speak English and were even taught our slang. They shot and killed our GIs as they approached. Behind these murderers were several divisions of German regular army. The SS troops took no prisoners. As we took prisoners we learned more about their dirty methods behind this maneuver. Some 200 German prisoners were ushered into our barbed wire compound. The snow crackled under our feet in the 30° below zero cold. The eight or ten MPs including me who staffed the compound were told of this dastardly German trick. We ordered the Germans to take off all their clothes and had them stand in the snow naked. A half hour later a general and his aides happened to drive by and seeing the naked men in the compound ordered us to have them clothed and ready to ship to the rear. He was furious as he observed the naked Germans. Some of the prisoners were so frozen they couldn't dress themselves and when the trucks came many were helped in, still naked. These Germans were a part of Hitler's SS troops. Hitler touted them as the Master Race. Let us not forget!

In any game or contest or fight and even in war I can see saluting the opponent; yes, even the enemy for his bravery, for fighting for what he thought was his right, but this was just plain murder. Shame on any of you who ever make an offer to honor these murderers. Christmas and new Years came and went like any other day. We're still trying to stay alive.

It was back to the Saar region to continue what we left before Luxembourg and Belgium and the Battle of the Bulge. The Siegfried Line and the crossing of the Rhine River contributed to many casualties.

Chapter 75

The stench of death is constant. Not quite as strong in winter, but it seems to linger from the warmer days gone by. Since it's now Spring the nauseating smell is overpowering again as we enter the small town of Ohrdruf.

Our heavy vehicles, churning up the road as we enter, unearth the worst this war has yet shown. For almost 150 feet of road, the earth still soft from a recent project, exposed the grave of murdered people. In their hurry to hide the crime before we got there, the long grave was too shallow to lessen the horrible smell. We immediately got some townspeople to begin to unearth this length of road. Major Couty sent two MPs to bring to this sight the mayor and his wife. Since I was the only one who spoke some German the major called for me to interrogate the mayor. He arrived with his wife the same time I did. He pointed to the end of the road where his home and office was and even though from the front of his house one could see clearly any activity down the road, the mayor insisted he did not know that these several hundred people were being buried here. It was easy to tell he was lying. The major placed him under arrest and two of our guys escorted the mayor and his wife back to his house. There was no way to prevent their actions. The mayor and his wife committed suicide minutes after being locked in their room. Only minutes later General Patton who was in the nearby area, arrived to witness the gut-wrenching picture. Of course, with him came the news people. Guess whose picture they took looking over the corpses?

Chapter 76

It was a little after liberating a women's concentration camp that I came down with a fever. I kept the dizzy feeling to myself for a few days until one of the guys noticed I wasn't too steady on my feet. He told Sergeant Newman, who, in turn, told Major Couty, who then ordered me to the hospital. I argued with the major about going and then came the direct order, a weapon a commanding officer has over an underling. I was pretty much in la-la land from fever, yet I heard but couldn't understand why, with a field hospital and station down the road, the major was ordering me to a waiting ambulance to take me to a hospital somewhere to the rear. The hospital I was being taken to was 400 miles away.

Between the fever and the knockout shot I got from our field hospital doctor, I don't remember the bumpy ride that took all night and part of the following morning. I'll never know why I had to go so far. I kept my gun with me as a matter of habit. No one ever touched my gun except the one time I let the major use it, and Anderson at Arniville.

In the hospital room, still groggy, I undressed, put my dirty mud encrusted clothes and gun in a closet. A nurse stood next to me the whole time. She had a pill in her hand and a glass of water in the other. The pill was bigger than any I had ever seen. I learned several days later it was called a Red 88, named after the German 88 millimeter cannon. I was put to bed without even getting washed. I was knocked out almost immediately and I slept for 24 hours or more. As I slept through the night I was given penicillin shots every three or four hours, never feeling anything. The shots continued for three days and whatever was wrong with me was cleared up.

It was on the afternoon of the third day I felt well enough to walk the hall outside my room. Part way down the corridor I noticed a small counter with candy bars laid out on top. A Red Cross girl sat beside the counter. Almost at the time I reached the counter, a soldier in a hospital gown and on crutches and with only one leg managed to reach the counter. He asked for a

Hershey bar. "That will be five cents," she said. The soldier answered, "I have no money." "I'm sorry," she said. The soldier turned and swinging his stump went back to his room. For a minute or two I stood there in such anger I could feel my fever coming back. I walked up to the counter and with the swoop of my hand brushed the counter top clean, scattering everything on it to the floor. The Red Cross girl, stunned with fear, ran down the hall and out of sight. I sat on the edge of my bed the rest of the afternoon, angry and depressed. He gave his leg - couldn't they give him the Hershey bar? For you believers, where is your God when you are in need? I guess I became the closest to being God for this amputee to show my wrath. My first thought was to pick up a candy bar and give it to the soldier. That would have been stealing and the penalty for that would have been worse than what I did. My demonstration was personal, but it should have been publicized somewhere along with the slap General Patton gave another victim of war. The next day, day four, a major walked into my room and said I was well enough to return to duty. I dressed in my old dirty clothes, shouldered my gun and met the major in the hall outside my room. "Who's responsible here for clean clothes?" I asked. He didn't bother to answer me. He wasn't wearing a medical insignia so there was no way I could identify him. He handed me a tag that had a number on it. The string on the tag was to tie around the button on my field jacket. From the hall window the major pointed to a large tent on the hospital grounds and said I was to report to the officer in charge there for further instructions. I stood outside on the top step of the hospital entrance for a few minutes. I stopped a soldier who was entering the hospital and asked him what the big tent was for. "A redeployment center," he said. I had heard of such a center before. It was for assignment to any outfit that needed men. Not for me was my immediate reaction and as I headed for the road I tore up my tag, scattering the pieces to the wind.

Chapter 77

I was heading toward the front, I thought since an old arrow nailed to a tree pointed in that direction and I hope my outfit. A good choice or a bad one, I felt that's where I belong. The 400 miles or more facing me were also frightening. I walked for many miles; I had no food, but I did, out of habit, fill my canteen with water before I left the hospital. The war, being so far away now, made me wonder if any vehicles used this road. Occasionally I would come upon an arrow nailed to a tree that pointed to the front with an insignia on it. I tried not to wander too far off to the side of the road for fear that mines had not yet been cleared. I decided not to walk at night so before dark I made sure the side of the road where I was going to spend the night was clear of mines. It rained the first night. That was the reason I didn't sleep. I walked most of the next day and late in the afternoon a truck, barreling down the road, stopped when I waved him down. It was a "Red Ball Express," but he wasn't going to the front. We rode some 50 to 75 miles when the driver said he had to turn off. He offered to take me along, but something told me to stay on the road ahead. I had one of the driver's C rations while riding and as I left the truck he threw me a K ration. I hated to ask for the one thing a soldier never parts with – toilet paper. He remarked that he too was in a similar situation at one time and understood the need. He handed me several pads. My only problem now is to keep them dry.

It was getting dark so again I bedded down on the side of the road. I don't think it will ever stop raining. On the following day a truck picked me up. He was headed for an occupation outfit some 100 miles down the road. It was chow time when we arrived and their field kitchen was serving their men. I waited till the line was through, all the time wondering what to say when I ask for some food. The mess sergeant looked me over. My MP helmet, arm band and my tommy gun may have looked impressive and he asked me where I was heading. "Fifth Division," I said. He said he had heard of us. Their uniforms were so clean I knew my muddy dirty clothes looked like I just

195

came out of a battle even though the fighting is so far away. I knew these guys had not seen any war because of their clean uniforms and I guess they had respect for those who had. "Eat all you want," he said. I took some leftover bread, stuffed my shirt pockets and took to the road. I did pass some farm houses, but I thought it best to keep to myself. I filled my canteen again at the field kitchen and the bread, if I can keep it dry, will hold me another day.

Three more days and nights of walking and I'm beginning to wonder if my choice to find my outfit was a wise one. There were a couple more short truck pickups, but all veering off to some other destination after 20 or 30 miles. I was quite weary after two more days of walking and just ahead, as far as I could see on both sides of the road, was some hilly terrain. I decided to rest at the bottom of a large mound just off the road. I finished the bread I had in my shirt pockets yesterday which was a bit damp from the sweat or rain that came through my shirt and tasted the same. My toilet paper is gone along with a shirt sleeve and the bottom part of my shirt that used to be tucked into my belted trousers. It was now day 10 since I left the hospital. I don't know how long I slept at the bottom of the mound. I was awakened by the sound of German vehicles. I knew immediately I was in enemy territory. The cold sweat and fear I've known for so many months and so many times broke out on me again. Except for the bottom of the mound where I was there was no place to hide. Suddenly I heard voices. The sound seemed to come from atop the mound. I thought for a moment and then decided to chance a look. I removed my helmet and I inched myself to the top of the mound ever so quietly and peered over the rim. No more than 20 feet away stood a German general and two of his aides. I inched my way down with goose bumps now growing among the sweat. There's no choice here for me to make, but to sit very still. I started to pay more attention to the terrain. To my left was a road that sloped down to a valley. It crossed the road I was walking on and seemed to come up to the top of the mound where the Germans stood. I could see down this road for half a mile. To my right were other mounds and some open fields. A half hour passed. I could still hear sounds of talking, but I couldn't make out what was being said. Suddenly, my trained ear heard a jeep in the distance. Looking to my left down the sloping road I could see the jeep and in a second or two the striped helmet that indicated they were MPs. Could they be my guys or MPs from another outfit? It didn't matter. They could be headed for a trap they're unaware of. I had only a few seconds to make a decision. In a flash and only a half minute before the jeep approached I scampered up the mound, my tommy gun pointing at the general shouting, "Hans a huff." The general and aides were startled as their hands bolted into the air. I suppose too the sight of my tommy gun was also frightening. If I did the wrong thing here a sniper or 50 others that had to be nearby will pick me off any second. I too was shaking and startled to see the jeep with the Fifth Division MPs as they rolled to my side. It was Sergeant Newman, Anderson and Pig. Pig yelled out, "It's the fuckin' duck." I didn't take my eye or gun off the general. Newman said, "we don't have time to hug you. Let's get these krauts back." The German general and aides were dressed and decorated like Christmas trees. Medals and other ornaments covered their chests. Newman said, "Let's disarm them and because the Duck came back to us, he'll get first pick." I called to Anderson to hold his gun on the general and at once apologized to Newman saying, "Sorry, Sarge. You're in charge," with Newman quickly saying "Anderson, hold your gun on the general." His glistening dagger, hanging from his shoulder fortiguere, looked like a suitable prize. With their weapons gone we all piled into the jeep, my tommy gun still pointed at the general. We headed back to division MP bivouac. I walked into the shack that was Major Couty's office. With such speed, his paw nails scratching the floor as he scampered, Luke lunged to greet me, nearly knocking me down. His whining and licking and pawing almost made me cry. The major made no attempt to call Luke off. I finally subdued Luke, saluted and said, "Reporting for duty, sir." The major looked at me for a full minute. None of the guys ever looked great, but I guess he wanted to see what 10 days like I must have had would produce. The major smiled and said, "Bunk down wherever you want." In reporting to the major regarding the German general and staff, Sergeant Newman related his finding me holding the German officers at gunpoint. The major himself never asked me to account for my 10 days AWOL. A lot of the guys gathered around me to hear my AWOL story while I devoured a ham and cheese C ration. The major let Luke run free, maybe to see what he'd do. He ran to where I was sitting and huddled down beside me.

Chapter 78

I learned quite a bit had happened during my ten day trek. The war was coming to an end and a cease fire is expected any time now. It accounted for the little traffic on my walking road and the reason for the turn offs of the few rides I got was because the road I chose led into the German territory. Most embarrassing of all was my holding up the German general and his staff at gun point. They were arranging for a surrender to us and were waiting for our MPs to pick them up. My action on that mound sounds more like a comedy, but I'm not laughing.

We were on the outskirts of a small town called Vilshofen. Our prisoner enclosure was very large, mainly because the thousands of Germans were trying to escape becoming prisoners of the Russians. On one occasion I walked into the enclosure to talk to some of the prisoners. The one American phrase they all learned was, "Me no Nazi." I wondered how that slogan was going over in the Russian prisoner enclosure. I wondered how Hitler would like to see his master race among the prisoners. Nothing was more in demand than toilet paper. That is somewhat of a victory for us, knowing how uncomfortable the super race must be feeling. I looked for a reaction from the prisoners around me so I said, "Heil Hitler." Groans came from some of them. One prisoner spit. I thought, not too long ago they were "Heiling Hitler" all over Europe and other places as he plundered and murdered.

Chapter 79

There are also quite a number of new men in our MP company and most of the assignments were being given to them. It was easy to tell them apart from the old guys. Their uniforms were so clean.

An order for the Fifth Division came. We're going home. We hoped this wasn't again only another rumor. The major called me to his office to remind me that I had more than enough points to be separated from the army here and now. I asked the major his opinion about my best chances of getting back to the states if I accepted discharge here or if I stayed with the Division. "Well, we're still at war with Japan and you never know what the army will decide to do. There could be a transportation problem and if you take the discharge here you could be stuck here in France waiting for a ship." I thought for a moment and said, "I'll stay with the division." With that the major handed me my corporal stripes and said, "You've been promoted." "Wow, with my record I don't know how this could have happened." The major didn't respond to that.

I started to salute and leave when the major continued, "The Division was ordered back to Le Havre. The greatest part of the division will return by train. I suppose it will be a cattle car. If you wish you could take a jeep to drive back. Choose three men and Luke." It didn't bother me at all that the major was thinking mostly of Luke. I would have thought the same. "We leave tomorrow. Get those stripes sewn on before then." I sought out the medics and with a needle and sutures I managed to get my stripes on. I chose Sol, Angelo and Chapman and that evening I loaded the jeep with C rations, water and extra gas. The trip to Camp Lucky Strike in Le Havre would take three days and in the early morning, even before the division departed, we hit the road. Of course, Luke sat up front with me. The ugly part of our trip to Le Havre was at stops and even on the way as Frenchmen cursed us out loud and yelled, "Yankee, go home!" We couldn't believe how fast the gratitude had vanished. We still had our guns and kept them displayed, hoping we wouldn't have to use

201

them if these lousy people got uglier. We slept along the side of the road next to the jeep. I was the warmest with Luke lying close to me. Hardly anyone was in Camp Lucky Strike when we got there. I don't know why this area was called a camp. There were no housing facilities. We lived and slept out in the open like we did through the war. Our field kitchen was still with the main body of the division and, like our war days, we continued to live on K rations. I and a couple of guys still had some C rations like ham and egg so we pooled them for Luke.

The camp was about a mile or two from the docks and it overlooked the ocean. We could see a ship if and when one came. The train carrying the division had an accident on the way and it took them five days to reach our camp.

The days dragged. Boredom began to feel worse than war. Angelo came by to express his gratitude for choosing him for the jeep trip. We sat under a tree staring at the ocean, recounting some of our experiences. We hadn't seen each other since Pienens, the girls and the canned spaghetti incident. "I told you, Angie. "Nothing to worry about." Angie smiled, his face was not as round as it used to be, but the dimples were still there. Looking up at the sky I said, "It just dawned on me that since Normandy I never saw a bird." Angie said he never gave it a thought, but thinking back, he agreed. I came back to my tree many times, still looking for a boat and writing letters. It's just possible I could get home before my letters.

I can't help thinking of the experiences I had with the different teams in my outfit.

We had deaths and dozens of horrible close calls and yet, with the exception of Captain Couty's promotion to major in the field and Sergeant Arndt's field promotion to second lieutenant, there were no signs of rewards in our Fifth Division MP company. No one was singled out for anything they might have earned for a mission or a job well done. But I knew why. It had to be recognized and accepted by the hierarchy. With the rivalry that existed among the higher brass there just wouldn't be any recommendations. Oh, yeah, no thanks to the higher ranking officers of the Fifth Division, we (every soldier that fought with us) earned a Silver Star. It was for five major battles; Utah

202

Beach in Normandy, The Hedgerows, Metz, The Battle of the Bulge and the Siegfried Line. I'll always remember.

There's nothing uglier than war, but there are times and people that make it necessary. We depend on our leaders to make sure people like Hitler never return. It's our responsibility to never forget. Leaders and important people make statements during the height of excitement and discussion. You want to believe a great leader, especially one who has earned his popularity through his deeds. And for me, General Eisenhower became that trustworthy person. It was especially at a time we were living in fox holes. Our Stars and Stripes newspaper rarely got to the front lines and if and when one did (and I mean only one), we would manage to pass it from fox hole to fox hole. This issue had a most important message to the armed forces in the European Theater. General Eisenhower said, "We will turn Germany into a farm land for them never again able to make war." When the guys were able to talk about it, we all approved. I hope I can trust Mr. Eisenhower to keep his word.

We awoke the next morning to a wonderful surprise. Our ship had docked during the night. The major and I met in the field not to be overheard by anyone. "You'll have to find a way to get Luke on board without anyone seeing you. This ship is under Navy command and the order is if any animals are found on the ship they're to be thrown overboard."

An armored unit would be the first to board the liberty ship. Supplies, then the men would be the last to board. The information came from reliable sources, total boarding would take four days. Security wasn't so necessary at this time so at 3 AM on the third night, still during the total blackout, Luke and I, unseen, strolled up the gangplank and made our way to Hold No. 1. I bedded Luke down on a blanket between two Sherman tanks. I then emptied my canteen of water in my helmet and wedged it between a box of ammo and the tank track. I stayed with Luke that night to help him become accustomed to this hiding place. I have always been an animal lover; as I said before, I never owned a pet and I never knew how to care for a dog, but I always thought these animals could sense being loved. Luke's intelligence, as intelligence goes for a dog, has been beyond description. I don't know when Luke began to understand English, but he began to respond even more some two or three months ago. He must have learned something from the major. He behaved properly with just normal conversation. And so when I said to Luke he had to be very quiet he looked at me and lay down on the blanket.

I managed to be present for roll call in the morning. It was this day the division was to board the ship. The hot breakfast of eggs, army style, and sausage from the field kitchen was a welcome and rare change, even a la Joe Moss. I told the major I'd be spending most of the time in Hold No. 1 with Luke and that, so far, there were no problems. I did learn from bull sessions in the past with the guys that sausage was not good for dogs, but for now I had nothing better. Luke gobbled them up and I accepted his muted whimper as "thanks."

At midnight we all felt the ship move. A feeling I longed for so long ago. Sitting with Luke between the tanks I wondered why, if we're heading for home, do we need all this hardware. The major could be right. You never know what the army will have us do when the brass upstairs finally decides.

On night three at sea I began to worry about Luke. Since day one he hadn't relieved himself and not a whimper from him. If the environment had an effect on him I decided to chance taking him on deck. Luke hugged my side quietly as we went from our hiding place to the outside.

With the ship being so crowded I knew we'd be seen by our men, but my biggest fear was the Navy guards. On the way up to the outside deck I asked several GIs to join me to form a screen telling them why I needed them as we walked. They were happy to do their part. I guided Luke close to the rail. It only took a minute and the operation was over and successful. How Luke knew this was the time I'll never know. It was so dark on deck we couldn't even see one another. With an old wet shirt in the dark I cleaned the area and kicked the shirt into the sea. It rained hard in the early morning so I knew any traces of Luke were gone. It was two nights later that I dared to take Luke up on deck again. This time we were caught. The partial moon made us visible. As the Navy guard and I stood facing each other and not saying a word, my mind was racing with options. I finally spoke just above a whisper. "If you make any move to take this dog I'm prepared to take you with us." It may have been a choice the guard didn't expect. Except to balance ourselves with the roll of the ship we stood very still. I could sense the guard was trying to decide what to do. It seemed like forever, waiting to hear him say, "I didn't see anything."

Our ship was timed to arrive in New York harbor in daylight and this time I was awake to see us sail by the Statue of Liberty.

Luke and I with the rest of the division walked down the gangplank to waiting trucks in full sight of everyone. No one could hurt us now.

Every division outfit assembled alongside the waiting train for roll call and boarding. Joe Moss and his food spoilers were there handing out cheese sandwiches -- one slice of cheese between two slices of dry bread. Swallowing wasn't easy.

Chapter 80

Camp Campbell, Kentucky is my final home.

After the very necessary shower I joined the long line at the bank of telephones to call Mom. Out of courtesy we all kept our conversation short. Knowing Mom, she wouldn't be completely happy and satisfied until she could see me and count for herself the arms, legs, eyes, etc. to be sure the whole Martin had come home. For me it was back to the end of the line again to call Mitzie. The first few days were spent at the canteen, listening to the juke box music, coffee and doughnuts and civilian sandwiches. I weighed 127 pounds and I hoped I'd be able to greet Mom without looking like a war atrocity. I believe the army's system of discharge was alphabetically. Sol and many others have already left. The camp was beginning to thin out. The barracks where I was living was almost empty. Luke slept in the bed next to mine, sometimes on the floor just next to my bed. It seems he can't get close enough. One of his intelligent show-off tricks, and he must have learned it by watching guys in the bathroom, was to open the faucet with his mouth to get a drink of water. When he was through he would leave the water running as it must have been too difficult for him to turn it off. I was getting edgy and bored with nothing to do so the major suggested I become the company mailman. It was good for a couple of hours each day. Luke was my assistant. He sat in the passenger side of the jeep and accompanied me on my rounds. I would sometimes forget and talk to him as though he were a real person sitting beside me. It took two weeks for my name to appear at the office that was responsible for my discharge. It was a decisive and a happy/sad morning when the major called me to his office. "I have your papers here and I have to ask you if you decided to take Luke home with you." I knew, back in Germany, when the major first rescued Luke, that he loved and wanted him. As close as I have become to Luke, I always felt he was the majors dog. It was thoughtful and generous for the major to think of me on such an equal basis. The lump in my throat began to swell. I was finding it hard to utter a sound. I knew I was going to give up Luke. It took a full minute for me to say, "My mother and I live in a small apartment. Luke needs lots of room." I took my papers from the major. As I shook his hand, Luke who was lying on the floor behind the major's desk, stood up. I stepped back, saluted, turned and walked to the door. I looked back at Luke. He must have seen me do this a number of times before, and had no idea that this was the final goodbye.

Chapter 81

I stood at the camp entrance waiting for the bus to take me to Knoxville, Tennessee to catch the train that will take me home. I looked back towards the barracks and down the streets, watching the vehicles rolling in all directions like it was once upon a time, and wondering if it's really over.

There's no way I could judge the time I would arrive home. I'd have to resort to an almost surprise.

Chapter 82

Mom always left the outside front door unlocked during the day. She always said security wasn't the most important thing in her life. Besides, Lynda, the owner of the beauty shop under our apartment, checked on Mom several times through the day. I walked up the stairs and opened the unlocked door that led to the kitchen and there she was. She said nothing while she hugged the whole 127 pounds of me. She gently moved me away for a second look. My gaunt face couldn't hide anything from her. "Look," I said, "two eyes, two legs and two arms." And with that arms outstretched, I hugged her again. Mom scanned my skinny frame and said, "You must be hungry." While I ate we sat and talked like we did a thousand times before. I tried to talk about some fun things, about some of the guys, about my friend, Sol. She knew I wouldn't tell her any war stories. "Mitzie called this morning to find out what time you would be arriving. Did you call her?" "No, I didn't. I thought I would just walk in on her." That's how it happened. The "Welcome Home" banner that stretched across the dining room wall had to be called to my attention. As large as it was, I only saw Mitzie standing in the doorway. There was, of course, a party that night. They just had to have one and although I would have preferred not to have any celebration, I thought they should be allowed to do their thing. It was early morning when I got home, only to find Mom waiting for me. The breakfast she was preparing for me was going to spoil me all over again, and again we talked.

I stood by the window looking out on 11th street and the few stores I could never forget were still there. The deli across the street – how many times have I thought about that deli? I'll be going there soon, even if it's just to smell the pickles and cold cuts and the hot rye bread.

Jack was home on furlough and Roslyn had come from Tampa to visit. Jack had fought the battle of Boca Raton and Miami Beach. There would be plenty of time to swap stories.

Joan was 15 years old and like a lot of kids her age she had trouble keeping a secret. Things she had overheard in family

211

conversations were reaching an explosive stage for her. Momentarily, when no one was in the room leaving us alone, she whispered to me, "Are you going to marry Mitzie?" I was at a loss for words. Mitzie and I, unknowingly, were maybe years ahead of society's mode of living. In all the years we knew each other, we were just good friends. I wanted her so much so many times, but war made us both think about "What if?" like not making it home again and if I did, in my case, with a mother to take care of. Whatever reasons Mitzie had, would have for her been equally important. So we never thought of or considered being engaged. If engagements are meant to be a time to know the other person before marriage, I believe the seven Marty-Mitzie years would be more than required.

I had the whole next day to spend with Mom since Mitzie had to go to work. I started the conversation by inviting Mom to a movie. "Not today,' she said. "I would like to talk about you and Mitzie." I thought about Joan's inquisitiveness pushing her to the point of calling Mom to find out what she knew. "What are your plans?" Mom asked. "Well, first I'm going back to work. The Marine Corps Quartermaster offered to reinstate me, but warned that with the war in Europe ended and the war with Japan probably coming to an end soon, there may not be a job there in the near future. I'll make other plans while working at the quartermaster." "I mean," Mom said, "are you and Mitzie going to marry?" "I don't know if I have the right to ask her," I said, "I want to be sure you will be taken care of and I don't think she should have to share in that. Besides, there's no hurry. I'll give it some thought when it's possible to be better prepared with a steady job and that may take a little longer." I could tell Mom was having trouble with this conversation because of her probing. "I thought about it for a long time," she said. "I didn't want to be the reason to keep you from living your own life. I married Uncle Joe two months ago." I guess I was visibly stunned. "I hope you won't be angry with me," she continued. "I could never forget the life cousin Morris had or should I say the life he didn't have. I couldn't let that happen to you. Anyway, it's done."

I left the living room to get a glass of water, but mainly to try to calm down. On returning I asked, "Where is Uncle Joe now?" "We have an apartment and he's living there now. I needed to be with you when you came home and he said he understood." It took several days for me to overcome the difficulty of accepting what Mom did and why she did it for me, but like she said, "It's done."

The owner of the apartment we were living in on 11th Street called to say he would like to have the apartment. He agreed with Mom to wait until I came home, but said he needed the apartment now. I prevailed when I asked him for an additional 30 days.

Mitzie and I continued to date. We visited Sol and Sophie in New York one weekend – separate rooms at the Edison Hotel – and we got to see the show, "Carousel." There isn't a second that I don't think of wanting Mitzie forever. I spent the biggest part of my young life in poverty, always looking for a job. Even the few good times came to an end with not too much reserve to feel comfortable. For Mitzie, I had to be sure we'd never return to those days.

The when and how escapes me. I only remember Mitzie saying "Yes" when I asked her to marry me. That was, I thought, all that was necessary, but Mitzie said it would be nice if I asked her father for his daughter. I thought we had outlived that muddle, but Mitzie said she knew he was expecting it and wanted to favor him in this wish.

Everyone was overjoyed by our decision. Roslyn who was the oldest of the sisters took charge of the wedding arrangements. One arrangement they couldn't make was a place for us to live. I had no idea that the war caused a shortage in housing too. A special government department was formed to allocate vacancies as they became available. For Mitzie and me this presented a serious problem. I couldn't blame her. Mitzie didn't want to live with my mother in her new and larger apartment, even if it would be a temporary arrangement. The wedding is off. It was late and there would be no trolley car for more than an hour so I decided to walk the three miles home. Walking and thinking sometimes helps, but this was a problem I was unable to solve. Rosalyn was more upset than we were. A few days went by and Mitzie called to say Ro had convinced her that the apartment problem shouldn't stand in the way of our getting married. I agreed.

Chapter 83

The wedding was a little bigger and more than I would have liked, but I went along with the affair, counting the hours and minutes when it would be over.

Ro described her home town and a beach resort in the nearby town of Clearwater on the Gulf which she thought would be suitable for our honeymoon. Mitzie and I agreed and we made reservations for a private room on the train. Ro and her daughter, Janet, who was 3 years old, took the same train home.

On the train that night I took from my suitcase the bottle of champagne I had carried from Rhiems anticipating this moment. Another little surprise for Mitzie and to tell her how I came to keep it all these past months. I peeled the wire and metal foil from the bottle. We both stood behind the bottle and easily pushed the cork, awaiting the pop. The pop was tremendous and the gush of champagne that followed came with such force it sprayed us and the entire room. When calm took over the surprise, only a quarter of a glass of champagne was left.

We laughed and, soaking wet, toasted each other for a fun life.

The End

ABOUT THE AUTHOR

Martin Tucker was born and reared in Northeast Philadelphia, Pennsylvania of Russian immigrant parents on February 11, 1917. He couldn't speak a word of English when he started school but battled his way through the early years. It was the Great Depression years that forced him to drop out of school so that he could earn enough money to help keep his family alive. The impressionable, invisible scars of the Army and the horrors of World War II are still imbedded in him never to leave.